BRITISH RAILWAYS

PAST and PRESENT

COLOUR SPECIAL
Second selection

WILLENHALL, WEST MIDLANDS: In this first *Colour Special* 'out-take' - from *British Railways Past and Present No 5: The West Midlands* - we see not only railway renewal, but also urban renewal, as the area's 'Black Country' tag becomes ever more inappropriate. Willenhall, situated between Wolverhampton and Walsall, is famous as a centre of lock-making. For a period the town also had two railway stations, at Stafford Street on the Midland line from Walsall, which closed to passengers in 1931, and at Bilston Street on the Grand Junction from Wolverhampton. The latter closed in 1965, when the local passenger service was withdrawn. Some years earlier a two-car DMU is seen departing from Bilston Street with a Wolverhampton High Level to Burton-upon-Trent (via Walsall) service.

The line today is used mainly by freight and weekend passenger diversions, the latter because it is the principal diversionary route for the West Coast Main Line when the Trent Valley section is closed. In May 1987 a southbound diverted express passes the site of the old station, hauled by a since-withdrawn Class '81' electric locomotive. There is much evidence of new high-rise housing and associated landscaping - but note how little the factory premises have changed.

Peter Shoesmith/John Whitehouse

BRITISH RAILWAYS
PAST and PRESENT

COLOUR SPECIAL
Second selection
including Irish railways
Plus 'Railway Signalling Past and Present' by Adrian Vaughan

Past and Present

Past & Present Publishing Ltd

First published in January 1995

The black and white 'out-take' photographs are previously unpublished 'past and present' scenes that the authors were not able to include in the volumes concerned, while the colour material is that added to the new editions of British Railways Past and Present Nos 5, 6, 11 and 19, and that contained in Nos 21, 22, 24 and the first volume on Irish Railways.

British Library Cataloguing in Publication Data

A catalogue record for this book is available from the British Library

ISBN 1 85895 072 4

Past & Present Publishing Ltd
Unit 5
Home Farm Close
Church Street
Wadenhoe
Peterborough PE8 5TE
Tel/fax (01832) 720440

Printed and bound in Great Britain

THE SEVERN VALLEY RAILWAY (P&P No 5): Even the longer-established preserved railways can now provide dramatic 'past and present' comparisons. In May 1970 the SVR ran its first train from Bridgnorth to Hampton Loade, and in the course of the following years it gradually extended the line southwards, finally reaching its goal of Kidderminster in 1984. On the second day of operation from Kidderminster, 31 July, 'Hall' Class 4-6-0 No 4930 *Hagley Hall* departs with the 6.08 pm to Bridgnorth. Only the platform is in situ, with one face in operation.

In time the excellent facilities now provided were put in place; first the impressive terminus station building incorporating a booking hall, public bar and bookshop. The building is based on a Great Western design, as is the signal box, which can be seen on the right of this May 1994 scene, taken during the annual diesel weekend; visiting Class '40' No 212 is departing with the 17.30 to Bridgnorth. Recently the railway purchased the freehold of the station site from the BR Property Board. Note that both faces of the island platform are now open. *Brian Robbins/John Whitehouse*

INTRODUCTION

'**S**omething old, something new' could well be the motto of this second *Colour Special* selection, for it blows the dust off black and white 'out-takes' from past volumes, as well as featuring the brand new colour photographs that have been added to eight new and recently reprinted volumes.

We start with the 'out-takes', a small selection of 'past and present' pairs that couldn't be accommodated in the volumes for which they were intended. This time they take us from the south-west of Scotland right down to the South Coast at Southampton, and even over the water to Ireland, whose fascinating railways are featured in the first of our new 'Irish Railways Past and Present' volumes.

Later we take a special look at an area of our railway heritage that is attracting an ever-growing following - signalling. Renowned railway historian Adrian Vaughan, himself a former BR signalman, explains the changes that have overtaken signalling at Westbury and Exeter, changes that are mirrored all over the country as traditional mechanical semaphore signalling is progressively replaced by electric multiple-aspect installations.

Opposite you will see two photographs portraying a decade in the life of one of our principal preserved railways, reminding us that even lines that have been 'preserved' have not been 'embalmed' - they continue to evolve and develop as did their eminent ancestors. As many of you will know, preserved lines are providing Past & Present Publishing with a further series of 'Specials', looking at the past and present of our best-known steam lines. Indeed, in many cases there are two 'pasts' - the pre-preservation scene and the post-closure 'limbo', when only the vision and sheer hard work of the preservationists was to ensure a 'present' scene of rebirth, together with a secure future. The first book in this series looked at the Paignton & Dartmouth Steam Railway, the next will cover the Severn Valley Railway itself, and several more are in preparation.

During 1995 the 'British Railways Past and Present' series will arrive at (and pass) its 'quarter century' - 25 volumes, featuring hundreds of locations and thousands of miles of railway from Perth to Penzance, Holyhead to Hastings. The books are not only a tribute to the photographers of the Steam Age, but also the tenacity, enterprise and skill of the present-day authorial teams. They also of course owe their continued success to you, the readers, without whom the series would not have remained a best-seller for a decade or more. So in placing on record our appreciation of the tremendous amount of work that goes into them, and the support of our loyal and much-valued readers who make it all worth while, let's raise a glass to the next 25!

Finally, a rather different and evocative perspective of 'past and presenting' comes from Ken Groundwater, co-author of No 11, *North Yorkshire Part 1*, with sentiments echoed later by Adrian Vaughan. When you have read the following, look at the pictures of the Settle & Carlisle line in the colour section included here, and I defy you not to hear the wind sighing in the telegraph wires. . .!

'In the mid-1960s, and penniless,' he writes, 'I walked the S&C route on many weekends and slept in p. way huts or disused signal boxes. Occasionally I found the funds to tape some sounds at the lineside. One such recording was made after waking (perished) at the disused Denthead signal box one August dawn. When I listen to these tapes today, it is noticeable how many more atmospheric sounds were about then.

'The majority are inevitably bird sounds associated with those parts (it *never* seemed boring up there between trains!), but also unmistakeable was the amount of sound associated with the telegraphy systems connected with the railway. It was noisy! My Denthead tape is special because of this otherwise forgotten memory, and if we could do *sound* 'past and present' the comparative silence today would be underlined.

'Gone now are the human "twitterings" heard from the "omnibus" phones then stringing together all the boxes in a particular circuit. In Denthead box the conversations passing backwards and forwards through that long night were between the signalmen of Dent, Blea Moor, Selside and Horton boxes. At one point all might chip in, while at other times just two held staccato conversations. And just when you thought both had nodded off, one would chirp up with a comment about so-and-so further down getting a new posting, etc.

'These air-waves from the past, coupled with the "wild harp" telegraph music and the sound of constantly tumbling water from gills and potholes (there was *always* a background sound of water, and shoes were always damp. . .) are like ghostly scratchings on my recordings. The sound was quite disconcerting on my first night, as the gurgling would intermix with the telegraph voices and produce a sort of spectral humming as if something or some-one was about to materialise, but one rapidly got used to it and accepted in all simply as a characteristic of the line.

'Today there are no sounds of signalmen asking "How's she deeing on t' up along" - and where's the water gone? On recent visits, the once notoriously boggy Blea Moor was in danger of going up with a single wayward cigarette end.

'There are fewer lapwing and curlew, but one thing remains constant - the noise of lambs. One silence different from the film!'

Will Adams
Editor

KILLINEY (Irish Railways P&P): The section of line between Dalkey and Killiney is probably the most photographed in Ireland - on one side is the sea, on the other some of the most desirable property in the country. No A13 approaches Killiney with the 17.52 Connolly to Bray in August 1971.

The 'present' view shows that the line is now electrified; a Bray-bound DART passes the same spot in August 1993. The Greek-temple-like building with the pillars set on the hillside belongs to Bono of the pop group U2, Bernard Shaw lived a bit further up the road, and numerous other famous artists and writers, including James Joyce, have also had homes in the vicinity, and there are a number of embassies set amongst the trees of Killiney Hill. It is not fanciful to compare Killiney with the French Riviera. *Both Michael Baker*

BARNESMORE GAP (Irish Railways P&P): A train from Ballyshannon and Donegal Town steams through the Barnesmore Gap on an unknown date. Having reached the summit of this lonely stretch of line it is taking a breather as it descends towards Stranorlar and Letterkenny. The three carriages immediately behind the 2-6-4T are of particular interest, being the finest built for ordinary service on the Irish narrow gauge. They originated on the NCC, being constructed in Belfast in 1928 for the Ballymena-Larne boat trains. Two of them were 50 feet long over the headstocks, and all three had corridors, gangway connections and electric lighting.

The only sign in August 1993 that a railway had ever run through Barnesmore Gap might seem to be a dip in the coarse, boggy grassland. *Michael Baker Collection/Michael Baker*

NEWTON STEWART (P&P No 19): BR Standard '4MT' No 76073 approaches Newton Stewart with a mixed freight from the west on 9 July 1963.

Thirty years on there is no sign that a railway ever existed here. The bridge that carried the road over the railway, from which the 'past' picture was taken, has been removed, and the road is now at the former track level. The only linking feature is the undulating wall across the field in the distance. *Michael Mensing/Keith Sanders*

ARTHINGTON (P&P No 11): In the mid-1950s Class 'D49' 'Hunt' 4-4-0 No 62727 *The Quorn* drifts into Arthington with a Leeds-Harrogate stopping train. This was one of the original two 'Hunts' to have the Lentz rotary cam valve gear. Originally called *Buckinghamshire*, she was renamed in May 1932.

In September 1989 a Class '144' unit passes the same location with a Leeds-Knaresborough train. The only link between the views is the telegraph pole - which is still leaning. The '8¼' milepost applies to the main route, and has usurped the '½' milepost on the now closed and removed spur towards Ilkley at this once triangular junction.
J. W. Armstrong/Alan R. Thompson

HEMINGBROUGH (P&P No 11) is on the Hull-Selby line, on the fringes of this volume's area. Some time in the mid-1950s Class 'B16' 4-6-0 No 61459 passes bound for Selby with a stopping train from Hull to Leeds.

The station is now closed and the platform removed, but in 1990 the station buildings still remain, as does the signal box, which is still in use for the road crossing and still controls manual semaphore signals. A Class '158' unit heads past with a Hull-Manchester service. *J. W. Armstrong/Alan R. Thompson*

LLANDUDNO JUNCTION (P&P No 6) once had its own locomotive shed and carriage servicing facilities, as pictured in this latter-day steam view dated 30 May 1966. The locomotive on the turntable on the right-hand side is Class '5' No 45284, while parked between two rakes of wagons is an English Electric Type 4 diesel-electric, one of the main classes of diesel used on the North Wales coast line until the 1980s.

By 1988 the locomotive shed has disappeared, giving way to earthworks for the new A55 tunnel. The carriage shed is still standing, although seeing only limited use compared with steam days. In the middle of the photograph is a rake of hopper wagons used to transport sulphur from Mostyn to Amlwch, a flow that ceased in 1989. *Wyn Hobson/Paul Shannon*

GREAT MISSENDEN (P&P No 24): On 2 July 1960 Fowler '4MT' 2-6-4T No 42256 arrives on a down stopping train bound for Aylesbury.

Goods facilities were withdrawn in July 1966, and the site of the former goods yard was later reclaimed for car parking, just as it was at so many locations in the Home Counties. The early 1990s then saw the long-awaited 'total route modernisation' of the Chiltern lines, bringing with it a new generation of rolling-stock as well as complete resignalling and various station improvements. Passing the now disused signal box on 13 February 1994 is Class '165' 'Turbo' unit No 165022, forming the 14.34 Amersham-Aylesbury local service. *Tom Middlemass/Paul Shannon*

SALISBURY SHED (P&P No 22): The driver of Class 'T9' 4-4-0 No 30707 climbs into the cab in order to back the locomotive down to the old Salisbury shed coaler on 13 May 1958. Salisbury shed was coded 72B in BR days and closed on 9 July 1967.

The shed was demolished in November 1969. The present-day photograph taken on 21 February 1994 shows in the bottom right-hand corner only the retaining wall of the coaling stage behind the 'T9'. The area is now overgrown with small bushes and scrub. Considerable clearing of these was required to obtain this view.
Brian Morrison/Graham Roose

GRAFTON & BURBAGE (P&P No 22): The neat layout looking south shows the station building and signal box on the down platform. The signals at the time of this photograph, 8 July 1954, were of Southern upper-quadrant pattern. The track to the right, alongside which there is a small loading platform visible by the loading-gauge, formed a loop behind the up-side platform.

Photographed again in November 1993, the modified and extended station building and canopy are seen to good effect from the attractive setting of a landscaped garden. *R. C. Riley/Graham Roose*

FARNBOROUGH NORTH (P&P No 21): The ex-South Eastern & Chatham Railway line from Redhill, which runs along the Surrey Hills, passes through both counties covered by this book, Hampshire and Berkshire. Farnborough North is in Hampshire, and on 23 March 1964 Class 'N' No 31869 arrives with the 16.20 from Reading to Redhill.

The regular service is now operated by DMUs, with all-stations trains running between Reading and Redhill, and fast trains between Reading and Gatwick Airport. InterCity trains to and from the north are also occasionally routed this way, instead of the more usual route via Kensington Olympia and Clapham Junction. On 4 April 1993 the 08.50 Liverpool to Poole rushes through Farnborough North ahead of time hauled by an unidentified Class '47'. *Both Terry Gough*

SOUTHAMPTON DOCKS (P&P No 21): Two Class 'USA' tank engines, Nos 30073/69, pause on the line running between the side of Southampton Terminus station and the Docks; this was the route that boat trains took to reach the Ocean Terminal. By the time this photograph was taken in 1964, new diesel locomotives built especially for the Docks had displaced most of the 'USAs'. In the background is the Terminus station concourse and the South Western Hotel.

The 1993 scene is little different, as the station forecourt canopy and the hotel (now called South Western House) are listed buildings. Although the line to the Docks is still in place, no trains have passed for many months and it seems unlikely that it will be used again. *Both Terry Gough*

Past and Present Colour

The West Midlands

ALREWAS is situated on the Lichfield line, close to the junction with the main line from Birmingham to Derby at Wichnor. The station served a rural area of north Staffordshire, and was a casualty of the Beeching cuts when the passenger service from Lichfield to Burton-upon-Trent was withdrawn in 1965. On 4 June 1963 Stanier '8F' No 48522 hauls a coal train through the station heading south. The signal box indicates clearly the LNWR ancestry of the line.

The line remains open today, principally as a freight line as far as Lichfield, which is the northern terminus of the Birmingham Cross City commuter line. The route is also used for weekend Inter-City diversions when engineering work closes the main line. In March 1994 the diverted 11.00 Derby-Birmingham New Street service eases over the level crossing headed by Class '47' No 47832. Some evidence of the platform remains on the far side. *Hugh Ballantyne/John Whitehouse*

BURTON-UPON-TRENT has long been associated with the brewing industry, and indeed remains so today. As the breweries developed, so did an extensive system of railways, with the town being served by the Midland principally, and also the LNWR, North Staffordshire and even the Great Northern. Around the breweries grew a web of railway sidings. Shobnall Wharf, located to the south-west of the town, contained one such concentration, with the railway forming an interchange with the Trent & Mersey Canal. At the nearby Shobnall Junction on 4 June 1963 ex-Midland '4F' No 44538 shunts, while alongside is Bass Brewery-owned 'Baguley' diesel shunter No 6. Note the Midland-pattern signal box in the background.

In March 1994 the location is derelict, the brewery railway system having been completely abandoned. *Hugh Ballantyne/Geoff Dowling*

WALSALL: On 4 August 1977 Class '47' No 47359 heads an Ironbridge-bound 'merry-go-round' (MGR) coal train through the station. At this time only the nearside platform was in use, for the electric service to Birmingham, while the platform and buildings on the left were used for parcels traffic and offices. The main booking hall, just visible above the rear of the train, was of an unusual semi-circular design with an attractive wood-panelled interior. When demolished during redevelopment of the site, the booking hall was donated to the nearby Black Country Museum at Dudley.

The redevelopment of the station can clearly be seen today, with a shopping complex now situated where the old booking hall stood. The left-hand platform building has been demolished, and now all platforms are in use following the re-opening of the Cannock Chase line to passenger traffic, presently to Hednesford, and hopefully later to Rugeley. The station still sees plenty of coal traffic, and Class '56' No 56065 also heads for Ironbridge with an MGR on 7 May 1994. On the right is a Class '310' EMU working the local service to Birmingham New Street. *Both John Whitehouse*

STOURBRIDGE TOWN is located at the end of a quarter-mile branch line from Stourbridge Junction station on the Birmingham to Worcester main line. On 19 May 1978 demolition of the old Great Western station had commenced with the removal of the canopy. Standing in the station is a first-generation single-car unit, a type that for many years was a feature on the branch. Until 1965 the line continued beyond the station to a goods depot, since when the area was redeveloped into the town's bus station.

In April 1994 the station area was again redeveloped, which included the provision of a new booking office and stop block, the latter designed to prevent further runaways following two such incidents in the past. The close connection with the buses remains to form an effective local transport interchange. A Class '153' single-car unit is now standard traction for the branch, as evident in this 28 April 1994 scene, just a few days after the new station reopened. In the current timetable there are 77 return journeys, each of which is booked 3 minutes between Town and Junction stations. *Peter Shoesmith/Geoff Dowling*

KINGS NORTON: An unusual combination of Type 2 and Type 4 'Peak' diesels heads a southbound express through Kings Norton in 1965. The station is of substantial size, befitting an important location in the southern suburbs of Birmingham. Immediately to the north of the station (beyond the background footbridge) is the junction where the line to Saltley via Camp Hill diverges from the Bristol to Birmingham main line. On the right is a diesel shunter, engaged in duties at the nearby car-loading terminal.

Today, not only has the station been rationalised, but also the Cross City Line electrification has changed the view significantly, although only the suburban lines, the nearest and furthest tracks, are electrified. On a sunny 25 April 1994 Class '43' No 43162 heads the 15.00 Newcastle-Plymouth IC125 service southwards. *Peter Shoesmith/Geoff Dowling*

TYSELEY: On 6 November 1965 Stanier '8F' No 48385 restarts an up freight from Tyseley. The station, of tradition-al Great Western design, is on the right, and consists of two island platforms linked by an enclosed footbridge that incorporates the booking office. To the left (out of the picture) is Tyseley locomotive shed.

Surprisingly little has changed, as this view taken on 26 April 1994 indicates. The station has been extensively refurbished, and the attractive 'Centro' livery is shown off to good effect on Class '150' 'Sprinter' No 150008, which is working the 13.12 Dorridge to Birmingham Snow Hill service. The city centre tower blocks can be seen on the horizon, and part of Tyseley diesel depot is just visible on the far left. *Michael Mensing/Geoff Dowling*

EARLSWOOD: The Great Western opened its North Warwickshire Line in 1908, which at long last gave the company an independent through route between Birmingham and Bristol, via Stratford-upon-Avon and Cheltenham. The line also became an important commuter railway, which is its principal role today. A number of stations were built south of Birmingham extending well beyond the city suburbs. Earlswood Lakes was one such rural station, seen here on 26 May 1964 in all its former glory with all station buildings and footbridge extant, as a three-car suburban DMU arrives with the 5.45 pm Birmingham Moor Street to Stratford-upon-Avon service.

Nearly 30 years later, on 18 March 1994, a new-generation DMU, a Class '150' 'Sprinter' in the livery of 'Centro', the local transport authority, calls at what is now simply Earlswood with the 15.22 Birmingham Snow Hill to Stratford-upon-Avon service. The station is now unstaffed and much rationalised, but the new M40 motorway is nearby, and schemes for a 'park and ride' facility have been mooted. *Michael Mensing/Geoff Dowling*

CLAVERDON station is situated on the branch to Stratford-upon-Avon, which diverges from the ex-GWR main line from Oxford to Birmingham at Hatton. The service in recent years has been sparse, although with the introduction of the new generation of 'Turbo Express' units, Stratford has at last acquired a regular direct service to London. On 15 May 1964 a three-car suburban DMU departs from Claverdon as the 7.36 am Stratford-upon-Avon to Leamington Spa (General) service. The unit is painted in the attractive green livery of the time, with white cab roof and half yellow front-end warning panel. Note that the line is still double-track.

On 30 April 1994 Class '153' single-car unit No 153381, in the most recent Regional Railways livery, approaches Claverdon with the 13.00 service from Leamington Spa to Stratford-upon-Avon. The track has now been singled, and the station, visible through the bridge arch, has been rationalised and is unstaffed. *Michael Mensing/Geoff Dowling*

Past and Present Colour

Cheshire and North Wales

CLIFFE PARK HALT was on the Manchester (London Road) to Uttoxeter route. On 30 September 1959 Fowler 2-6-4T No 42363 leaves with the 3.44 pm from Macclesfield (Hibel Road) to Uttoxeter. The station was situated in a very rural area and closed in 1960, although the line survived until 1965.

Today there is nothing left of the railway other than a footpath following the old trackbed, as seen in the modern picture taken on 17 July 1994. *Michael Mensing/John Hillmer*

ALTON TOWERS: Ex-LMS Fowler 2-6-4T No 42323 arrives with the 11.25 am Leek-Uttoxeter train on 19 August 1961. Situated on the scenic Churnet Valley line, the station closed in 1965, but as can be seen in the 'present' picture, taken on 9 July 1994, it remains in excellent condition. *Michael Mensing/John Hillmer*

KIDSGROVE was located at the junction of the lines from Manchester to Stoke-on-Trent and the branch from Crewe. The 'past' picture shows two two-car and one three-car Birmingham RCW DMUs forming the 1.45 pm Llandudno to Derby service passing through the station on 26 September 1960.

As can be seen, there have been a number of changes since. The line has been electrified, and the gasometer has gone, as has the brick building on the up platform together with that on the down platform to Crewe. The 9 July 1994 picture shows Class '150' No 150120 in Centro livery forming the 12.18 service from Crewe to Nottingham. *Michael Mensing/John Hillmer*

CREWE: On 26 May 1960 Stanier 2-6-4T No 42590 stands at the south end of the station. It is likely that the train will run as empty coaching stock, leaving Crewe at 4.26 pm and forming a Radway Green ROF workers' train - it will reverse off the Crewe line at Kidsgrove and take the 'loop line'.

Despite a gap of 34 years, the 'present' picture, taken on 11 June 1994, shows little obvious change, although the station underwent a major rationalisation in 1985. Class '156' No 156404 leaves with the 14.17 to Nottingham, while on the right Class '90' No 90020, in RES livery, is stabled. *Michael Mensing/John Hillmer*

GRESFORD HALT was located between Chester and Wrexham on the ex-GWR line from Birkenhead to Shrewsbury. On Easter Monday, 18 April 1960, '4300' Class 2-6-0 No 7310 arrives with the 1.15 pm Chester to Wrexham General.

The station closed in 1962, but part of the station house was incorporated into a small modern housing development. The line is now down to single track between Saltney Junction and Wrexham, as seen in the modern, 9 August 1994, view. *Michael Mensing/John Hillmer*

WREXHAM: Ex-GWR 'Castle' Class 4-6-0 No 5019 *Treago Castle* passes Croes Newydd South Fork box with the 5.43 pm Wrexham to Shrewsbury on 18 April 1960. Very much Great Western territory, Croes Newydd steam shed was close by with an allocation of mainly freight locos. Above the roof of the second coach can just be glimpsed the gable end of a house, which is about the only way of locating the 'present' picture, taken on 19 July 1994. Trees prevent an exact replica, but a more elevated viewpoint reveals that the tracks are down to two, plus the entrance to Watery Road goods yard. *Michael Mensing/John Hillmer*

MOLD: Photographed on the last day of passenger traffic, 28 April 1962, BR Standard Class '4' 4-6-0 No 75033 is seen leaving the station with the 5.00 pm Denbigh to Chester General train. The railway from Chester to Mold dated back to 1849 and on to Denbigh some 20 years later.

After cessation of passenger services, the line to Mold remained open for freight, but now nothing remains. The site of the station is occupied by a Tesco store, as shown in the 'present' photograph taken on 19 July 1994. *Michael Mensing/John Hillmer*

RHYL: BR Standard Class '4' No 75039 approaches Rhyl with a down excursion on Sunday 23 August 1959 with 10 coaches of mixed maroon and 'blood and custard' liveries. Since then, the track has been reduced from four lines to two and considerably more building has taken place. The 'present' picture was taken on 19 July 1994 and shows the 13.24 Crewe to Bangor, formed of two-car units Nos 158758 and 156246. *Michael Mensing/John Hillmer*

Past and Present Colour

North Yorkshire

ARTEN GILL VIADUCT: 'WD' No 90243 plods north along the Settle & Carlisle line with the Widnes-Long Meg empties on 18 June 1966 in conditions that must have delighted if not surprised photographer Bill Chapman! This timeless scene is accentuated by the casual way that the plume of exhaust is thrown over the shoulder of the locomotive; it almost seems as though it could have been photographed yesterday.

In fact, little has changed by 'yesterday' - July 1994 - although the passing of the pole-route seems in some way to have reduced the drama of communication aspects here on the roof of England. *Bill Chapman/Peter J.Robinson*

RIBBLEHEAD: On the old Midland Railway 'up-along', 'Black 5' No 45228 rattles over the rail-joints leading into Ribblehead station. It is once again 18 June 1966, and incredibly this former main line, built on a bluff and ostensibly 'closing' ever since, was to see out British steam traction more than two years later. Behind the bush, in line with the viaduct, is hidden the Station Inn. This celebrated hostelry is steeped in railway lore and current owner Keith Coates is still adding to the Inn's trophies. However, who could forget the publicans during the 1960s - the Menheniotts? Their ability to produce curry and something 'medicinal' at all hours was socially extremely necessary, if not slightly illegal!

Today, the mass of Whernside continues to sulk behind, but is now eroded by the army of walkers that have passed since far-off 1966. *Bill Chapman/Peter J.Robinson*

DENT: On the same fine day in 1966 another 'Black 5' passes through with freight from the yards at Carlisle. Viewed from near the signal box, the cattle-dock and the then already 'distressed' snow fences are clearly on view. This notoriously windy corner would attract snow drifts up to bridge parapet height in bad winters.

Today the two firs stand witness to the passing of the Steam Age and sleepers (remains of the old siding) lie forgotten and unwanted as DMU No 156489 calls. *Bill Chapman/Peter J.Robinson*

PATELEY BRIDGE: Leaving the Leeds Northern main line at Ripley Junction, the Nidd Valley Line operated a passenger service from 1862 to 1951, and thereafter freight until 1964. On 11 March of the latter year, seven months before the last goods pick-up, 'K1' No 62046 (borrowed from York shed) takes some refreshment before embarking on the return journey to Starbeck, Harrogate, with just three of these vehicles. Note the footpath on the extreme left sandwiched between the River Nidd and the station.

By July 1994 the old Goods Dock has been conveniently built up into a large retaining wall supporting new gardens, and the car threat is seen to have triumphed completely over the territory of its old adversary. The large station house (seen in *Past and Present* No 11, page 57) is not visible in this view. Steps now run down to the footpath, and because of the rich foliage we have compromised a little to give a meaningful view rather than simply a tree trunk! *D. J. Mitchell/Peter J. Robinson*

MELMERBY, junction for the Masham branch, was first proposed as the NER's gateway to Hawes and the Midland Railway, and would have looked a good bit different had the plans succeeded. Then the branch line, shown here sidling into Melmerby from Masham with a lowly D3872 at the head of the goods, would have been far more conspicuous. However, it was not to be, and shortly after this photograph was taken in November 1963, the branch closed for ever. Pulling away from the camera and into seasonal mists is a Leeds to Darlington DMU with a next stop at Northallerton.

In July 1994 a small boy plays on the old 'down main' line; further comment is perhaps unnecessary! *D. J. Mitchell/ Peter J. Robinson*

RICHMOND: This photograph of the station provides an intermediate view to those on page 44 of *Past and Present* No 11. It is now 1964 and here is the successor to the Class 'A8' and 'L1' tank engines. All but two of the five roads remain, while the NER ground signal has been replaced by the modern BR circular 'dolly'.

Another 30 years rolls on and the neatly installed garden centre now has a most established look. This was a station. . .? *D. J. Mitchell/Peter J. Robinson*

YORK (WATERWORKS CROSSING) was so called from the collection of white buildings that sat in the 'V' of the crossing, which housed pumping equipment to provide water for railway use. They are obscured in this view by 'A4' 'Pacific' No 60022 *Mallard* and her train, and it is fitting that she is pointing somewhat symbolically towards her final resting place. Few, if any, of those glancing from behind their newspapers would have been interested in their motive power; their thoughts instead might have been 'is this old boiler going to get us home. . .?', for by this date (April 1963) diesel reliability was increasing dramatically.

Today *Mallard* is blue and No 4468. . .and just around the corner in the National Railway Museum. The tight curve off the 'Scarborough' into platform 9, together with the huge 'block' crossing, have been replaced by an altogether simpler layout, and a colourful collection of units compares unfavourably with the drama that has now gone for ever from this location. *T. J. Edgington/Ken Groundwater*

YORK STATION SOUTH: Standing in the shunt bay that is now platform 7 at York is Class 'J72' No 68736. She was one of two that got favourable treatment in 1960 in response to a request that some NER apple green would not come amiss around the place. Upon becoming redundant here No 68736 joined her apple green sister at Newcastle until their end came in 1964. Few would argue that this wasn't a nice touch, although those that remember them perhaps also remember treating their ever-presence with some contempt.

Today it is certain that visitors to York would welcome the sight, but Railtrack might have other ideas! Modern canopies, lighting and nameboards have replaced the older examples and the water column, and the empty goods yard in the background tells its own story. *E. E.Smith, Ken Groundwater Collection/Ken Groundwater*

Past and Present Colour

South West Scotland

CRAIGENHILL: On 21 September 1963 two Clayton diesels, Nos D8522 and D8546, approach Craigenhill Junction with an up freight. This junction was situated halfway between Carluke and Lanark Junction, and the short branch served a lime mine.

The 'present' picture, taken on 1 November 1994, shows that the signal box has long gone, and the tree growth has hidden any sign of the branch trackbed. A railway telecommunications tower has been erected on the down side. *W. A. C. Smith/Keith Sanders*

BEITH: On 15 September 1962 one of the two Bristol/ECW railbuses stands in the Caledonian and Glasgow & South Western joint station at Beith. This was the terminus of the short branch from Lugton.

The scene on 17 September 1994 is much changed, as the whole station site is now a housing estate. Careful investigation does, however, reveal the ornate chimneys of a house in the background of both pictures. *Douglas Hume/Keith Sanders*

MONTGREENAN: On 21 July 1973, because of engineering works in the Glasgow area, which prevented direct access from Glasgow Central to the West Coast Main Line or to the Kilmarnock line, trains were diverted via Paisley and Dalry in order to reach Kilmarnock and the Sou'West line. English Electric Type 4 No D412 is seen passing the site of Montgreenan station with the 14.05 Glasgow Central-London Euston service.

On 1 November 1994 the trackbed is clearly visible, and behind the trees the station building is still standing and in use as a private residence. *Douglas Hume/Keith Sanders*

PORT GLASGOW: Stanier 'Black Five' No 45360 calls at the station in early 1962. This picture was taken from a footbridge that ran across the west end of the station.

The footbridge no longer exists, nor does the bay platform, so a slightly different position had to be adopted for this view of unit No 303087 departing for Gourock on 1 November 1994. On the hillside one block of flats has been demolished, but otherwise there has been little change to the surrounding buildings. The red board on the platform is the back of a large mirror so that the driver can see down the train for 'driver only operation'. *W. A. C. Smith/Keith Sanders*

PAISLEY GILMOUR STREET: Fairburn 2-6-4T No 42264 restarts the 3.15 pm Glasgow Central-Wemyss Bay service from Gilmour Street on 29 September 1962. The grimy condition of the locomotive and station was so typical of the time.

By comparison, the present-day scene is quite colourful, with unit No 316267 departing for Gourock on 1 November 1994. The station has received new awnings, and even boasts plants around the bases of the lighting poles. *W. A. C. Smith/Keith Sanders*

PAISLEY ST JAMES: The 'Jones Goods', Highland Railway 4-6-0 No 103, is seen in charge of one of the famous 'Easter Rambler' tours on 17 April 1965 while covering the Renfrewshire lines.

Today the station is unstaffed, and accommodation for passengers is provided by a small 'bus shelter' on each platform. On 1 November 1994 unit No 318265 heads for Glasgow Central. Many buildings in the area have been demolished, which adds to the feeling of dereliction. *Douglas Hume/Keith Sanders*

MAXWELL PARK: BR Standard 2-6-4T No 80002 accelerates the 6.12 pm Glasgow Central-Cathcart 'Inner Circle' train away from Maxwell Park station on 12 April 1962. Upon withdrawal from active service, this locomotive was used as a stationary boiler at Cowlairs Carriage Depot. From there it was saved from being cut up and is now at the Keighley & Worth Valley Railway awaiting restoration.

On a rather dull 2 November 1994, electric unit No 303040 gets under way in virtually the same surroundings. The absence of the white building on the right-hand side is the major change. *W. A. C. Smith/Keith Sanders*

IBROX EAST JUNCTION: BR Standard Class '4' 'Mogul' No 76001 works a freight train off the Govan branch at Ibrox East Junction on 29 September 1962.

Thirty-two years on, only the gas-holder and the low retaining wall remain from the 'past' picture. Ibrox station closed on 6 February 1967, and the present-day simplified layout of just two lines came with the electrification of the line. Unit No 303034 heads for Glasgow Central on 1 November 1994. *W. A. C. Smith/Keith Sanders*

READING (SOUTHERN) MPD: 'West Country' Class No 34037 *Clovelly* graces the shed on 15 December 1963. The GW main line is on the left, and the SR terminus some distance behind the camera. The gas works is visible in the background beyond the shed.

Redevelopment of the site makes exact location of the spot difficult, but a gap in the industrial buildings that now occupy the former SR territory enables an almost matching view to be obtained. The signals controlling the WR main line and the gas holder in the background confirm the location in March 1994. *Hugh Ballantyne/Terry Gough*

SOUTHCOTE JUNCTION, just south of Reading West, is readily accessible by a public footpath that gives good views of trains on both the Basingstoke and Newbury lines. On 4 July 1959 'Castle' Class No 7022 *Hereford Castle* approaches the junction (the line on the right is not the Basingstoke line, but a spur to Central Goods).

The Central Goods line has been taken up, but the other two lines are still heavily used by both passenger and freight trains. On 17 March 1994 Class '59' No 59001 *Yeoman Endeavour* takes an empty stone train back to Merehead Quarry. *R. C. Riley/Terry Gough*

NEWBURY EAST JUNCTION was the point where the Didcot, Newbury & Southampton line from Didcot met the GWR main line between Newbury and Newbury Racecourse stations. On 7 July 1956 Class 'T9' No 30289 brings the 15.40 Didcot to Southampton Terminus train round to the junction.

There is no trace of the junction in this 1994 view, but the houses in the background act as a marker. 'Thames Turbo' No 166206 forms the 13.31 Paddington to Bedwyn train on 10 March. *R. C. Riley/Terry Gough*

HUNGERFORD: Excellent views of the railway could be obtained from Hungerford Common. On 4 July 1959 'The Royal Duchy' heads for Cornwall behind 'Hall' Class No 5976 *Achwicke Hall*.

Nature has since blocked the view, even in winter when this photograph was taken, and now it is only possible to get a glance of trains from the other side of the line. The view from the bridge in the background is also still clear, and photographs from there are included on page 122 of 'BR Past and Present' No 21. *R. C. Riley/ Terry Gough*

BASINGSTOKE (1): 'Warship' Class diesel-hydraulic locomotives were used on the South Western main line to Exeter following the end of steam. No D801 *Vanguard* waits to leave Basingstoke with a down train on 1 April 1967.

Almost 27 years later to the day at the same spot Class '442' 'Wessex Electric' No 2418 forms the 11.48 from Waterloo to Poole. The water crane, already superfluous in the 'past' photograph, has been removed. *Neil Davenport/Terry Gough*

BASINGSTOKE (2): Following the closure of the Somerset & Dorset line, the 'Pines Express' was routed via Basingstoke and Reading, and is seen at the former place bound for Manchester on 1 August 1964. The locomotive is 'Merchant Navy' Class No 35005 *Canadian Pacific*.

There are now many more workings from the South of England to the North, and even in winter there is a bi-hourly service through Basingstoke. On 17 March 1994 an 'InterCity 125' waits for a door to be closed before heading for Edinburgh as the 11.20 from Bournemouth. *Neil Davenport/Terry Gough*

WINCHESTER CITY: The road overbridge at the south end of the station gave an excellent view of the railway. On 24 June 1957 Class 'M7' No 30376 heads towards Southampton Terminus with a local train.

A visit in the winter is now necessary to obtain a clear view of the station, and this was the scene in early 1994. The platforms have been lengthened and both platelayers huts have gone as a 'Wessex Electric' pulls out of the station forming the 08.05 Waterloo to Poole train. *R. C. Riley/Terry Gough*

EASTLEIGH: A view known to thousands of railway enthusiasts - this is Eastleigh seen from the road overbridge that led to the Works and engine sheds; the Carriage & Wagon Works is in the right background. 'West Country' Class No 34012 *Launceston* works the 08.30 from Waterloo to Bournemouth on 30 August 1965.

There is now far less traffic than in steam days, but Eastleigh is still a very interesting place to visit. In mid-March 1994 'Wessex Electric' No 2417 forms the 09.48 Waterloo to Poole train. *Hugh Ballantyne/Terry Gough*

Past and Present Colour

Wiltshire

HIGHWORTH: The little market town of Highworth lies some 6 miles to the north-east of Swindon. The railway was promoted by the Swindon & Highworth Light Railway, but like so many Victorian railway enterprises, it failed before it was able to complete its line to the satisfaction of the Board of Trade Inspecting Officer, so it fell into the hands of the Great Western and was opened to public traffic on 9 May 1883. This was the terminus station of the branch, 5½ miles from the main-line junction and situated on a rising gradient of 1 in 203, at the top of an even sharper rise of half a mile at 1 in 44. This picture shows part of the simple wooden station building, goods shed and diamond-pattern blue brick platform paving as Class '03' D2195 climbs into the station with the unadvertised evening workmen's train, the 5.28 pm from Swindon, on 18 June 1962, six weeks before closure.

By April 1994 all trace of the station has gone, and the area now forms a residential area known as Home Farm Estate. This photograph is as near an approximation as possible to the 'past' picture. *Hugh Ballantyne/Graham Roose*

SWINDON STOCK SHED, on the north-east side of the vast Swindon railway complex, was situated near the locomotive depot adjacent to the line to Kemble. It was designed for storing motive power and rolling-stock, although in later days it was used for holding engines awaiting a decision or scrapping. When this picture of No 1003 *County of Dorset* was taken on 20 September 1964 the locomotive had been withdrawn for two months, hence its sad appearance without nameplates, numberplates or connecting rods. The Dynamometer Car, No W7W, had been built at Swindon in 1907 for use in road-resting locomotives to measure their effectiveness as power units. The car was used in the well-known Locomotive Exchanges of 1948, but in 1961, when a replacement was built, W7W was retired. It is seen here stored out of use pending scrapping, but fortuitously it was subsequently saved for preservation and is now safely installed on the Dart Valley Railway. Part of the gas works built and owned by the GWR is visible in the background, with the largest of four gasholders, of 2.5 million cu ft capacity, prominent. This works was closed in January 1959 and supplies subsequently obtained from the South Western Gas Board, who took over that particular holder.

Development has completely transformed the locality by April 1994, but the gasholder remains, its top just visible left of centre, albeit now storing natural gas rather than manufactured town gas. *Hugh Ballantyne/Graham Roose*

MALMESBURY was reached by an independent company that built a line from the GWR main line at Dauntsey, a distance of 6½ miles, which opened on 17 December 1877. Not surprisingly, the company was taken over by the GWR in 1892, and following the opening of the South Wales direct line from Wootton Bassett, the branch connected with that line at Little Somerford, and eventually by 1933 the shortened branch of 3¾ miles came into use, and the section to Dauntsey was closed. As seen here on 12 June 1962, goods traffic continued to thrive and the yard was busy, particularly with loads of farm machinery from Messrs Blanch, so much so that implements were parked on the station platform for loading. Class '03' diesel shunter D2187 is seen at work shunting past the station platform. The attractive Cotswold-stone-built station is still complete with its canopy, although the bay windows are boarded up. On the left the small single-road engine shed, closed in 1951, has lost the track leading to it.

While one would expect that the splendid but partly ruined Abbey church, clearly visible in both pictures, would continue to dominate the landscape, surprisingly the little loco shed also survives in February 1994, albeit reno-vated and with the ends filled in, and now serving as part of a small tyre-fitting business. The trackbed, station and goods yard have all been swallowed up by redevelop-ment as an industrial estate, and a mature tree has grown up in the position once occupied by D2187.
Hugh Ballantyne/Graham Roose

HOLT JUNCTION station was unusual in Wiltshire, being a small country station comprising an island platform only. It was also in an isolated location some way from the nearest habitation. The railway from Thingley Junction was opened in 1848, but it was not until the line to Devizes was completed in 1857, making its junction here, that a station was constructed, which opened with the Devizes branch on 1 July 1857. It was simply an interchange station with no access to or from the village, unless one walked for a mile across the fields. Eventually in the 1870s a road was made and a goods shed constructed, so the station was then able properly to serve local needs, albeit that passenger access to the platform was by means of a footbridge from the north-west side. On a warm summer's day, 10 August 1963, No 6968 *Woodcock Hall* arrives at the station with a holiday train, the Saturdays-only 11.10 am from Wolverhampton to Weymouth. The station was closed to all traffic on 18 April 1966.

The 11 April 1994 picture was obtained with the permission, help and courtesy of Mr Maurice Arlett, who pinpointed the 'past' location, as little now remains to make identification possible. However, with the aid of tall stepladders placed near the old station approach road where the footbridge had been, and the grass bank on the right forming the rubble/spoil of the demolished island platform, this photograph makes the nearest possible comparison. The surviving running line is that on the left of the 'past' picture. *Hugh Ballantyne/Graham Roose*

WESTBURY: A BR scene on 12 April 1982, when corporate blue for locomotives and blue-grey coaching stock liveries were de rigueur, and no exceptions to the rule tolerated. Even that dreary livery era has now become part of history, and this picture, taken only 12 years before the 'present' equivalent, can now never be repeated. Locomotive-hauled trains no longer operate Portsmouth to Cardiff services such as that seen here behind No 33048, and the semaphore signals and box were superseded by multiple-aspect signalling (MAS) on 14 May 1984. Westbury North box, with 99 levers, controlled the starting signals seen here, and the road is set as No 33048 pulls away from the platform; the distants belong to Hawkeridge Junction.

Nowadays the station, much rationalised trackwise and controlled by MAS, sees very few locomotive-hauled passenger trains. The scene today will produce Class '150' 'Sprinter' DMUs, such as seen here on 18 May 1994 in the form of No 150249 arriving as the 14.20 Swansea-Portsmouth Harbour. Westbury North signal box was demolished in May 1984. *Both Graham Roose*

FAIRWOOD JUNCTION, WESTBURY: This early BR diesel era scene shows blue-liveried 'Hymek' No D7033 passing the junction signal box and taking the Westbury station line with an up stone train comprising 21-ton capacity HOP wagons from Somerset Stone Quarries sidings on 12 July 1969. The signal box here was opened on 1 January 1933 when the Westbury avoiding line, seen in the foreground, came into use, forming one of the well-known GWR 'cut-off' lines built to provide faster through running to its principal destinations, in this case for services to the South West of England. D7033 was a 1,700 hp diesel-hydraulic built for the Western Region by Beyer Peacock in May 1962, but had a very short working life of less than ten years, being withdrawn in January 1972.

It is pleasing to be able to record one of BR's success stories, the introduction of company trains to haul block loads. This complete train, locomotive and bogie stone wagons, is owned by ARC Ltd and painted in that company's livery, and is seen also taking the Westbury line with a load of roadstone from Whatley Quarry, North Somerset. The locomotive, No 59102 *Village of Chantry*, is a 1990-built General Motors 3,300 hp diesel-electric, one of four owned by ARC. Although the track layout remains the same as in the 1969 picture, the signals and box have gone; the latter was closed on 11 May 1984 when the MAS came into operation. *Hugh Ballantyne/Graham Roose*

WILTON SOUTH: Under clear signals from the down starter, with its tall post and repeater arm for sighting purposes, No 34091 *Weymouth* pulls away with the 11.15 (Sundays) all-stations Salisbury to Yeovil Junction local train on 23 June 1963. Just beyond the down sidings can be seen the bridge over the A36 Warminster Road.

No trace of the down platform or sidings remains, although the running lines are still, for a short distance, double track; the single-line section starts round the bend that the Class '159' unit is approaching as it passes by as the 16.30 Salisbury to Gillingham service on 18 April 1994. *Hugh Ballantyne/Graham Roose*

SALISBURY (SR) SHED lay to the west of Salisbury station, and was built by the LSWR as a substantial ten-road shed with its entrance facing east. It was an important shed in the Western Division of the Southern Railway and remained so in BR days, save that it was coded 72B, placing it in the Exmouth Junction (Exeter) group. The shed remained in use to the end of Southern Region steam, closing on 9 July 1967. When this picture was taken on 23 June 1963, except for the diesel shunter all the engines visible were Southern; left to right, they are Nos 35004 *Cunard White Star* and 'S15' No 30512 in the shed, while outside, tender leading, is No 34091 *Weymouth* with 'N' No 31813.

The shed was demolished in November 1969 and the cleared site remains an undeveloped wasteland overgrown with bushes and scrub. No remains of the buildings are visible on 21 February 1994. *Hugh Ballantyne/Graham Roose*

Past and Present Colour

Buckinghamshire, Bedfordshire and West Hertfordshire

ST ALBANS CITY: Recalling the long-forgotten days of 'Rail blue' and the inviolable BR corporate image, Class '45' 'Peak' No 45070 passes St Albans City with a 'merry-go-round' coal train for Northfleet cement works on 21 September 1979. The up side parcels dock is still in daily use.

Within a year of the 'past' photograph the scene had been changed by the erection of overhead catenary and the replacement of semaphores by colour lights. The parcels facilities were also soon to be withdrawn. No 45070 lasted until the mid-1980s in revenue-earning service, while the last feature of the old photograph to disappear was the coal traffic to Northfleet, coming to an end in 1992. The present-day scene shows Class '319' unit No 319030 departing as the 10.03 Bedford—Sevenoaks service on 29 March 1994. *Both Paul Shannon*

NAPSBURY is pictured on 17 September 1979, with preparatory work for resignalling and electrification in progress. Crossing over from the Up Slow to the Up Fast line is an engineers' train with Class '25' No 25277 at the front and sister locomotive No 25176 at the rear. The photograph emphasises the kink in the Up Slow line and the unusual positioning of Napsbury signal box, both brought about because there was once an island platform here between the two Slow lines.

No-one would ever guess today that there had once been an island platform station at Napsbury. A mid-morning InterCity 125 service for London St Pancras speeds past on 29 March 1994. *Both Paul Shannon*

LUTON BUTE STREET station is pictured on the last day of operation, 24 April 1965, with a two-car Cravens diesel multiple unit about to depart for Welwyn Garden City. The first DMUs had been introduced to the line in September 1962, just after the ex-LNWR section of the route from Dunstable to Leighton Buzzard had been closed.

In 1994 the motor car reigns supreme! The track through the former Bute Street station was removed in 1992, instantly stifling plans to bring the Dunstable branch back into use for steam locomotive crew training, and making it seem less likely that the branch will ever be reopened to passengers. *Stephen Summerson/Paul Shannon*

GREAT LINFORD: Long before this part of rural Buckinghamshire became enveloped by Milton Keynes new town, Ivatt 2-6-2T No 41222 sets off from Great Linford with the 1.30pm Newport Pagnell-Wolverton train on 26 October 1963.

In July 1994 the scene at Great Linford is still green, although the course of the railway is now flanked by a mixture of parkland and housing instead of farmland. The former trackbed has been made into a pleasant walkway and cycle track. *Michael Mensing/Paul Shannon*

LEIGHTON BUZZARD: Stanier '8F' No 48550 comes off the Dunstable branch with a short mixed goods train on 1 May 1963.

Thirty-one years later all traces of the goods yard and branch line to Dunstable have long since vanished. The growth in long-distance commuting from the 1960s onwards is shown graphically by the number of cars in the car park, as well as by the lengthened station platforms. *Stephen Summerson/Paul Shannon*

WATFORD JUNCTION: Stanier rebuilt 'Royal Scot' 4-6-0 No 46146 *The Rifle Brigade* storms through Watford Junction with a lengthy up parcels train on 27 October 1962. No 46146 was withdrawn from stock only a few weeks afterwards, its West Coast Main Line duties taken over by diesels until the completion of electrification in 1966.

Watford Junction station was rebuilt and the footbridge removed in the mid-1960s. The result is a rather nondescript but functional modern station, now overshadowed by a 1980s office development visible on the far left of the photograph. A '92xxx' Driving Van Trailer heads the 15.30 Manchester Piccadilly-London Euston service into the station on 17 June 1994, with a Class '90' locomotive bringing up the rear. *Stephen Summerson/Paul Shannon*

BICESTER NORTH: 'Hall' Class 4-6-0 No 4907 *Broughton Hall* arrives at Bicester North station on 31 May 1960 with the 4.34 pm semi-fast train from London Paddington to Wolverhampton High Level. This train waited at Bicester until the passage of the 5.10 Paddington-Wolverhampton express, which had a slip coach dropped from it for attachment to the 4.34 service.

The same view is illustrated on 24 March 1994, with Class '165' unit No 165026 pulling away from Bicester North as the 17.30 Banbury-London Marylebone service. Goods facilities were withdrawn from Bicester North in 1964, and in 1968 the line was singled except for a passing loop in the station. After 1968 the 'North' suffix was no longer necessary, as Bicester's other station, on the ex-LNWR route to Oxford, had closed down, but the suffix was reapplied in 1987 when passenger services to Oxford resumed. *Michael Mensing/Paul Shannon*

CHESHAM: Although the Chesham branch was never owned by British Railways, trains on it were hauled by British Railways locomotives until the commissioning of electrification in 1960. The live rails provide a contrast with the water crane in this view of the Chesham terminus dated 21 August 1960. Ivatt 2-6-2T No 41284 is just arriving with the branch train from Chalfont & Latimer.

Much rationalisation and modernisation has taken place at Chesham by the date of the second photograph, 13 February 1994. A train of A60 stock arrives with the 14.00 departure from Chalfont. *R. C. Riley/Paul Shannon*

Past and Present Colour

Ireland

DUBLIN CONNOLLY station, formerly Amiens Street, at dusk on 22 December 1981. The passenger walking away from the camera is standing on what used to be the edge of the Howth bay platform, then recently filled in. To the left are the through platforms of the once separate Dublin & South Eastern station, to the right the former Great Northern Railway's terminus.

On a bright March morning in 1994 we can see that the semaphore signals and signal box have gone. The former DSER station was completely rebuilt on the inauguration of the DART suburban electrics in 1983. In the former GNR station is an Irish Rail '121' Class diesel-electric, and, further down the line, a Northern Ireland Railways '111' Class Co-Co. *Both Michael Baker*

EAST WALL JUNCTION, DUBLIN: The Belfast-bound 'Enterprise', the 11.00 from Connolly, passes East Wall Junction in August 1969. The 'Enterprise' is the generic name for all through passenger expresses between the two capitals. The seven-coach train is headed by '70' Class diesel-electric railcar No 77, built three years earlier. These Ulster Transport Authority (UTA)-designed units had then recently taken over from GNR ones.

The 'Enterprise', now timed to leave Connolly' at 11.20, passes the same spot on 31 March 1994. The locomotive is No 113 *Belfast & County Down*, a 2,250 hp General Motors Co-Co diesel-electric, introduced by Northern Ireland Railways in 1984. The carriages are BR Mark IIb's and one Mark IIc, put into service at various dates from 1970 onwards; the livery dates from 1989. The tower of Connolly station and Liberty Hall, Dublin's highest building and the Trades Union headquarters, appear in both pictures, but the signal box and semaphores of 1969 have long gone, and the supports and overhead for the DART electrics are now prominent. Fluorescent jackets would not have been around in 1969. *Both Michael Baker*

HOWTH JUNCTION: A Drogheda-bound morning commuter push/pull train made up of converted Park Royal railcars, propelled by a 'B201' Class Bo-Bo diesel-electric, stands at the down main platform in December 1981. The tracks curving away from the junction are those of the Howth branch. Beyond are flats and houses dating from the expansion of the Dublin suburbs northwards in the post-war years and immortalised as Barrytown by Booker-Prize-winning author Roddy Doyle.

On 31 March 1994 a Dublin-bound suburban train composed of Craven carriages built between 1963 and 1967 stands at the up main line platform in the charge of a General Motors '141' Class Bo-Bo. Since electrification of the Howth branch it is no longer possible to exactly repeat the previous shot, for the sides of the footbridge from which it was taken have been raised and covered in. Gone are the palm trees, the semaphores and the signal box; the concrete suburbs beyond are unchanged. *Both Michael Baker*

DUN LAOGHAIRE PIER station on an August evening in 1979, with a 'B201' Class Bo-Bo, a Metro-Vickers design dating from 1957, re-engined by General Motors from 1970 onwards, about to depart for Pearse, Connolly and Heuston stations, Dublin, with a boat train. Standing alongside is the 7,839 gross ton Sealink ferry MV *St Columba*, dating from 1977.

The railway closed in 1980 and the track was taken up, leaving intending rail passengers either a long walk, laden with luggage, to the main-line station at Dun Laoghaire, or a ride on a double-deck bus, ill-equipped to carry luggage, to the city stations. On the evening of 28 March 1994 the ship is the same, but now renamed *Stena Hibernia*; it is due to be replaced by a vastly bigger ferry, but there is much controversy whether this should use an enlarged Dun Laoghaire Pier, disgorging more and more cars and juggernauts on to the town's inadequate road system, or be transferred to the North Wall, Dublin. *Both Michael Baker*

MULLINGAR: Moving west now, to the former Midland Great Western line from Dublin, we visit Mullingar on an icy cold December day in 1979. A '001' Class is about to depart with the 08.20 Dublin to Galway mail. Although a weak sun shone, the temperature remained below freezing point all day.

No trains are to be seen nowadays, for all Dublin to Galway and Westport services go by way of the former GSWR main line as far as Portarlington, and no regular traffic disturbs the rust-covered rails between Mullingar and Athlone. Otherwise, on 2 April 1994 nothing much seems to have changed; there is even a covering of white, a freakish spring snowstorm having just swept over the surprised inhabitants of Mullingar. Beyond the station at the junction with the Sligo line can be seen two carriages belonging to the Railway Preservation Society of Ireland (RPSI), which has its southern headquarters here. *Both Michael Baker*

LISTOWEL was on the former Limerick-Tralee line. Passenger services ceased in 1963, although an occasional freight or passenger special still passed this way when this photograph was taken in August 1978. The signal box, although boarded up, is intact; beyond are the station buildings and footbridge. The donkey is standing where the Listowel & Ballybunion monorail, which closed in 1924, used to curve in and run alongside the main-line station.

All that remained of Listowel station by 7 April 1994 was the ruined buildings on the down platform, the track having been lifted and the footbridge and signal box demolished - the frame can just be seen lying by the fence. I cannot say what happened to the donkey. *Both Michael Baker*

GLANMIRE ROAD, CORK: At the Cobh end of the station in August 1977 a Class '001' Co-Co is approaching with a freight from one of the yards further down the River Lee towards the open sea. A General Motors Bo-Bo is in the yard just behind the signal box, while beyond another '001' is just visible in front of the locomotive depot.

The same view in April 1994 shows that the signal box has been repainted and fitted with new windows, and all the nearer semaphores have been replaced by colour lights, although further on and down the Cobh they still flourish. The track layout has been simplified; on the far left stands an '071', while outside the depot are a couple of General Motors Bo-Bos. *Both Michael Baker*

BELFAST: Finally, Northern Ireland steam in service and in preservation. Former Belfast & County Down Railway 4-4-2T No 221 (UTA number) stands at Queens Quay, Belfast, after overhaul in 1953. No 221 was built by Beyer Peacock in 1921 and withdrawn in 1956.

An earlier example of the class has, however, been preserved. No 30, built by Beyer Peacock in 1901, is now to be seen in Belfast Transport Museum. *Colour-Rail/Michael Baker*

BRITISH RAILWAY SIGNALLING PAST AND PRESENT

Adrian Vaughan

The railway marked out the landscape, and not just with its embankments and its cuttings through a hill, the recognisably 'railway' fence-posts marching over the high field marking the line of route below ground. A railway line was 40 feet tall - even on a bridge above the line, the observer was still below the top of the sturdy, cross-barred telegraph poles with their tensioned, humming wires. And down the line a way there might be the white post and yellow arm of a 'Distant' signal.

Hanging over the bridge at a station the ornate chimneys came close below, while on the bank, to one side, water trickled endlessly, tinkling and hollow within a supply tank. It always ran, yet there seemed to be no overflow. There was enchantment in the mysterious, musical water and the humming wires.

A tall signal came up close to the bridge, the arm high to be seen from a distance above the cutting. The signal post, arm, lamp case and finial (or cap) had distinctive and satisfying style. Down below, the station also had a style that marked its company and its period; style in its tiles or slates, the way they were hung, style in its chimney stacks, style in the sort of guttering around the eaves. Somewhere nearby, right below the bridge if you were lucky, was the signal box. This too was full of character - and not just in its architectural style. The signalman, too, was probably quite a character.

His signal box might have dated from a quadrupling done in the 1930s, or from a new railway built around the turn of the century, or it might have replaced some ancient structure when the old company was feeling rich, usually between 1900 and 1914, or indeed it might have been as old as the railway. In the later 1930s, during the war and in the 1950s, progressive Signal Engineers tried their hand at some more modern manual signalling equipment in modern structures, and these have an unfortunate tendency to ugliness. However, generally speaking, the British railway scene in 1965 was as it had been in 1900. The 'furniture' was handsome, solid and built to last; some of it had lasted from 1875, and there was a great deal of it, from signal bells to buffer stops.

The signalman worked at his ancient skill with equipment that, even if it had been made in 1934, was shaped to designs dating back decades. Every 2 miles or so (and much less in towns) a signalman watched the trains, belled them on, saw trouble and tried to prevent accidents. There were a great many signalmen and enginemen, and, nationwide, a certain number of accidents each year. Some railways fared better than others.

The men worked for 20 days out of 21, 8 hours a day, early, late and nights, and 12 hours at weekends with less than the correct number of hours of rest between shifts. The latter was a matter so routine as to be ignored by everyone. The work could be heavy, physically as well as mentally. Many boxes never had running water or a lavatory; a spring in the field or running water to a cattle trough served for the former, and often water came in cans on the buffer beam of the local goods train. For a lavatory, well. . .

But it was a secure and satisfying job. The vast majority of signal boxes were in the countryside, and even some large junctions had nice views of fields. The signalmen were in charge of their patch. They made the decisions, and if anything went wrong the inevitable question was 'What shall we do, "Bobby"?'

Under semaphore signalling trains were inspected very frequently and could be pulled up quickly if there was trouble. If the line became obstructed, the obstruction could at once be protected. In 1966 a landslide blocked the line at Briton Ferry. It happened very close to the site of a signal box, so the earth would have prevented the signal wires from moving. Unfortunately the signal box and its wires had been abolished only a few days before. A parcels train, running under colour-light signals, ran into the obstruction and the driver was killed.

Communication between a semaphore signalman and a driver required that the train be brought to a stand and the driver 'advised'. This did waste time, but at least there was a signalman able to stop the train. Indeed, a signalman's job *is* to stop trains. Messages of the greatest importance from the driver or guard could be conveyed to the signalman from a moving train by wrapping and tying the written message around a lump of coal or a rolled-up timetable.

The first great change in the railway landscape was the removal of the telegraph pole routes in the 1960s. This reduced the height of the railway, in open country at any rate, to the height of a rail. The closure of stations and signal boxes followed on closely. Now there were the ulcerating eyesores of decaying, vandalised railway stations, where they had not been turned into potholed parks for heavy lorries or rat-run car scrapyards. Of course a few were saved to become private houses, and some of these sites are very fine indeed.

Signalling ceased to be handsomely Victorian and became instead brutally modern. Absolutely standard signals were placed at, say, 2,000-yard intervals, creating a hypnotic boredom for the drivers of high-speed trains, against which they had to fight hard, causing mental stress hitherto unheard of.

The look of layouts changed too, because the points were power-operated and did not have to be kept within 350 yards of the signal box, and also because the type of motive power changed. There was far less shunting to be done. Plain 'crossovers' were all that were required, replacing the visually very attractive 'single' and 'double' compound points, arranged as one piece or in that long sequence of complication known as a 'ladder crossing'. This is not to say that such pointwork does not exist under modern signalling, but rather that such devices are rare.

The buildings housing the signalling consoles may one day be seen as triumphs of mid-to-late 20th-century industrial architecture, but at the moment most of them look as if they will not last long enough to reach any venerable age. The modern power signalling control room is almost windowless; the operators look inwards, not outwards. It need not be anywhere near the railway line. It is efficient at running trains, until some tiny component fails. It is heavily supervised and bureaucratic.

The signalling system is as far as possible automatic, the signals changing with the passage of the trains and, in the most modern systems, operated by a computer programme. Here the operator's role is to watch until some malfunction, mishap or late running calls for his or her intervention.

Responsibility for safety under ordinary working conditions has been, to a very great extent, removed from the operator and put on to the designer of the circuitry and the manufacturer of the relays and other appliances. The maintenance technicians are more at risk of causing an accident than the operators.

But when the 'electrics' fail, then the operators have a very heavy responsibility for safe working because they have to over-rule the interlocking with verbal messages that they hope will not be misunderstood. Modern power boxes have tape recorders to record what is said on the telephone between signalman and driver (or whoever), which is a great assistance in working out blame after an accident but no use in preventing the misunderstanding.

The great failing of the power signalling schemes of the 1960s and '70s was in their lack of control over the signals and in the operator's remoteness from the scene of the action. Even if an operator was made aware of an obstruction, he might not be able to protect it because of his lack of control over automatic signals. After several narrow escapes the authorities put more signals under operator control. Today the greatest aid to control is the two-way radio between signalman and driver.

In August 1994 the signalman at York was able to warn the driver of an approaching HST that a runaway engine was approaching him - on his line. The HST driver had 2 minutes in which to stop his train and get himself out of the cab; the engine crashed into the HST without killing anyone. Undoubtedly the radio saved the trainmen's lives and perhaps those of his passengers also.

In the days of traditional signal boxes, a signalman would have been available to divert the engine to the right line and ultimately into the ground, harmlessly.

All photographs by the author unless otherwise credited

The first group of photographs looks at signalling changes at Westbury, Wiltshire. The first view is 250 yards from Westbury North in 1974, approaching the station on the line from Newbury. This track was known officially as the 'Patney' because it was from Patney that the route was constructed in 1900, a 'cut-off' from the old Newbury-Devizes-Trowbridge line; the Trowbridge line is on the right. The photograph shows a semaphore junction signal for a left-hand turn-out. The Distant signal is motor-worked from Westbury South box and could only be lowered after the upper, right-hand, stop arm had been lowered. If the upper arm was lowered but the Distant arm remained at 'Caution', it gave the semaphore version of a 'single yellow' in a three-aspect colour-light signal.

At approximately the same site in May 1985 are signals designed to be seen from locomotive cab height; from the ground their lights are dim. W298 (left) is a three-aspect signal with a left-hand junction indicator (the 'feathers') above it. Thus it corresponds to the pur-

pose of the previous semaphore signal. W198 (right) has a very compact four-way junction indicator. It is just possible to see that W298 is indicating a 'single yellow', with the 'feathers' alight for the turn-out, while W198 also has a 'yellow' and is illuminated for a right-hand turn. Alongside each main signal head is an elevated 'position light' with a duplex route indicator above. The signal gantry shows that either track can be used for entering Westbury station, rather than, in semaphore days, having only one 'Down' and one 'Up' track.

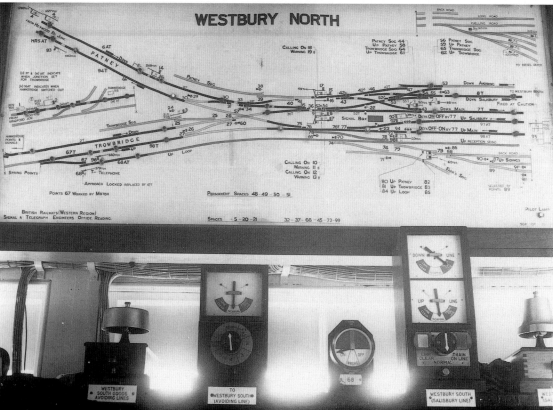

WESTBURY NORTH

Left A little further on we arrive at this semaphore gantry at Westbury North, with two, three-way, indications. Looking at the right-hand group we see that Westbury North's Down Main Starting signal (No 7 on the diagram reproduced below) and South box's Distant are lowered - a driver would understand from this that the road is clear as far as Fairwood Junction's Home signal. The next signal (No 8) routes from the Down 'Trowbridge' to the Down 'Salisbury' platform line, and the third (No 9) to the Down Goods Avoiding Line. The left-hand group of three read, from right to left: Down Salisbury to Down Main (No 16), Down Salisbury (No 15), and Down Salisbury to Down Goods Avoiding Line (No 17).

Below signals 7, 8 and 15 are 'subsidiary signals' with their oil-lamp-lit indicators. These show either a 'C' ('Calling-on') or a 'W' ('Warning') when the small arm is lowered. 'C' would be used for example to bring a shunting engine into an already occupied platform, while 'W' would be used if the approaching train had been accepted under the 'Warning Arrangement'. The driver would then understand that the line was clear only as far as the Home signal of South box and was blocked immediately beyond that. The indications given by these signals would in a modern system be given by a 'position light' mounted below or to one side of the colour-light signal head.

Below left The layout controlled by the Westbury North signalman in 1974. In the 'V' of the junction the layout controlled by Hawkeridge Junction signal box is also included because Westbury North shared control of Hawkeridge's Down Distant and Home signals; thus they appear on the North's diagram.

Above The nearest equivalent to a 'position light' in the semaphore signalling system is the disc signal. This could be used on the ground or in an elevated position for shunting movements. Here are front and rear views of a GWR cast-iron ground signal assembly carrying three Western Region-pattern discs in 1970. The triple-vertical assembly is the equivalent of a three-post bracket signal, and the configuration could route as follows: bottom disc, first turn-out left; middle disc, second left; top disc, third left. Or it could mean straight on, first left, first right. This is why drivers had to acquire 'route knowledge'. A modern 'position light' in this situation would have a route indicator giving precise information as to which route had been selected.

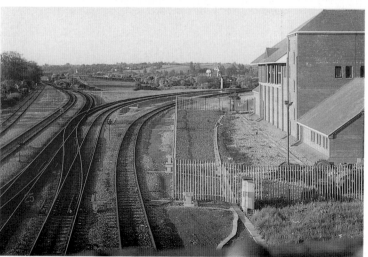

A rear view of the 'Salisbury' half of the gantry on the previous page, showing the Trowbridge line on the left with a Class '50' diesel in 1974. The Patney line disappears behind the Distant signal arm. 'East Chord', connecting the two routes, from Hawkeridge to Heywood Road Junctions, runs left to right on a level with the top of the Distant signal arm.

The view from the same site 11 years later shows the re-modelled junction that reflects the manner in which, with modern power signalling, trains can readily be allowed to run over either line in both directions. Such simple-looking layouts are in fact quite potent with a large capacity for trains. The new Panel Signal Box is on the right.

Westbury North signal box in 1974, with signalman Sid Fleming. The box is a GWR standard brick, hip-gabled design, opened with the new station *circa* 29 July 1900.

The box closed on 28 April 1984, and the replacement Panel Box building seen here in May 1985 is known to the inmates as 'Colditz Castle'. It was built with enough space to house all the panels ever needed by Western Region, but now that Western Region is no more, having been overtaken and disbanded by politics, the building may become an expensive 'white elephant'.

Westbury North box interior in 1974, with signalman Ian Wannell. There are 86 working levers numbered 1-99. A Westinghouse hand generator is nearest the camera, by the window on the left; this drove the exit points from the Up Goods Loop on the Trowbridge line. The box emergency lighting consisted of one Tilley paraffin pressure lamp and one ordinary wick lamp with a glass chimney. On 9 October 1978 a small panel was commissioned here to operate the junction to Salisbury and other features formerly controlled by Westbury South box. On 3 June 1979, Warminster box, on the Salisbury line, was abolished, putting the small panel in touch with Codford. On 22 June 1982 Codford box was abolished, bringing the panel in Westbury North box into direct communication with the large, new, Panel Signal Box (PSB) at Salisbury. *John Morris*

Westbury station was closed completely from 7 April to 13 May 1984 for track remodelling and signal box decommissioning. The new Westbury PSB came into operation on 14 May in the station area and to Salisbury; its sphere of operations was then extended in stages until, on 28 April 1985, it controlled the tracks from Edington & Bratton to Somerton and linked up with Salisbury panel at Codford. It replaced 14 signal boxes, counting from the musterroll of boxes in 1978. During the weekend 17-19 March 1990 Westbury PSB was extended to encompass Bradford Junction; it then worked with Reading, Bristol, Swindon, Salisbury and Exeter PSBs. In this 1985 view, Chris Burden is at the modern equivalent of the 'booking desk', and Bernie Miles is on the phone at the control console.

This is part of a GWR 'tappet' interlocking machine, which became standard GWR equipment in 1923. The principles of the design date back to James Deakin's patent of 1870. The machine is mounted vertically below the row of levers, which are in the room above. When a lever is pulled over, its tappet blade is driven downwards - by means of a cam plate attached to the lever - if the locking permits the movement; the ends of the cam plate can be seen at the top of the picture. Here, tappet blades 1, 2 and 3 are up, because their levers are 'normal' in the frame, but No 4 blade is down because that lever is reversed.

Note the notches in each blade to accommodate the locks. The vertical movement of the blade will displace the lock sideways, provided there is a space opposite into which the lock can move. If there is nowhere for the lock to go, the blade - and thus its lever - cannot be moved. The movement of the locks on these levers is transmitted to locks on other levers by means of the horizontal bars.

No 4 lever operates the Starting signal. While it is reversed, its tappet blade is down and its lock is displaced; that movement can be seen by the displacement of the horizontal locking bar out of register from the rest. This movement will have locked the 'main to main' crossover and several other points.

The second view is of the underfloor scene at Westbury Panel. The process of setting up a route is commenced by the operator pressing the relevant button(s) on the console. These relays deal with sending current out to the lineside interlocking locations, and receiving detection current back from points and signals to feed indications of the setting of points and signals on the Panel console.

Relays at the lineside site carry out the functions of interlocking - proving the track circuits clear and signals correct before switching current to the point motors. After points have 'motored' and have been proved through their detection contacts, an indication current is sent back to the Panel while other circuits are made to operate the signals, then further indications are sent back to the Panel.

When a train moves past the signals and occupies the track circuits beyond, it activates the relays to replace the signals to 'Danger'. However, the points do not move until the signalman instructs the machine to set a different route. This system of relay interlocking is old, dating back to 1923, and has since been superseded by the computerised 'Solid State Interlocking' (SSI). There is no visual similarity between the three systems - mechanical, electric relay and SSI - but the system of logic underlying all three is identical.

Westbury North box from the station in 1973, showing a GWR 'Backing' signal (nearest the camera) and a GWR-pattern, tubular steel junction signal. Both sets of arms are at equal height indicating that each diverging line has the same speed limit and is of equal importance. The left-hand Distant signal arm is operated from Hawkeridge Junction, the right-hand arm from Heywood Road Junction. The 'Backing' signal applies to a reversing movement out of the Down Main platform and has a mechanical route indicator to advise 'Patney Sdg', 'Up Patney', 'Trowbridge Sdg', or 'Up Trowbridge'. The specialised 'Backing' arm was abolished in 1949, but some examples survived into the late 1970s. This one was replaced in 1975 with an ordinary 3-foot arm; an elevated ground disc could also have been used.

The second view shows the equivalent colour light 'splitting' junction signal on the same site in May 1985. Mounted alongside is an elevated 'position light' and two route indicators. A Bristol-Salisbury DMU is arriving from Bristol on what would have been, in semaphore days, the 'wrong' line; it was routed this way to avoid obstructing the Down 'Patney' line on which was approaching a Paddington-Plymouth express. Station operation is made simpler by being able to come both in and out on one track.

Our final look at Westbury shows Middle box and the yards, looking south along the Up Salisbury line platform on a miserable December day in 1969. The left-hand arm of the signal on the down line routes from Down Main to Down Salisbury. There are subsidiary arms on each post; when one of these is lowered there is nothing visible to indicate to a driver whether it is acting as a 'Calling-on' or a 'Warning' signal. The stop signals are the Homes for this box, and are also the signals giving access to the section ahead. A driver must know this fact so that when a subsidiary arm is lowered he will understand that the section to Westbury South is clear but the line may be blocked at the latter's Home signal. The signalman, being equipped with these signals, will not give any other indication to the driver.

Looking south from near the same spot in 1985, the Bristol-Salisbury DMU seen opposite is leaving down the Up Salisbury with the route ahead set for the Down Main; it will turn on to the Salisbury branch at Westbury South.

No 50010 has arrived from Paddington almost at the same time as the DMU. Under semaphore working the latter would have 'crossed the bows' of the express at Westbury North to reach the Down Salisbury platform, and one or other train would have had to be delayed. Under the new system, using the 'wrong' line, neither were delayed. On the far right an elevated 'position light' is showing a 'proceed' aspect (two white lights) and its route indicator shows 'BK' for 'Back Road'.

We now move to Exeter St David's, in 1971 a conventional layout with a 'Down side' and an 'Up side'. This is the view from the West signal box. The Down Main line runs through the centre, between the right-hand (No 1) and central platforms (Nos 3/4). Platforms 1 and 3 are loops off the Down Main and are available for down trains. The Southern Region route from Waterloo is in the right foreground; trains for Waterloo gain access to SR metals off the Down Main and Platform 3, obstructing through trains approaching Exeter in the process (the points at the end of Platform 1 lead only to the 'South Devon Sidings'). Trains from Waterloo use Platform 4 (where the locomotive is standing), and also obstruct the whole 'Down side'. The Up Main line runs into Platform 5, with loops off this serving Platforms 4 and 6.

The 1985 view shows the simple modern layout for the same station, seen from the same vantage. The apparent simplicity, as at Westbury, is misleading. The layout has been re-vamped to be much more powerful with fewer tracks and 'wrong direction' working possible over all lines. The Up and Down Main lines now pass between Platforms 4 and 5; Platforms 1 and 3 are now to one side of the main lines, but up and down Western Region services can still reach them through facing connections from the main lines. However, the effect of the re-alignment of the tracks is to make Platforms 1 and 3 as good as a separate station, mainly for the use of Southern services, which can now come and go without any delay to 'main line' trains. One wonders why the GWR did not think of this improvement 60 years ago.

The view west along Platform 1 in 1974 over the Steam Age junction at Exeter St David's, unchanged for perhaps 60 years. The points at the end of Platform 1 lead only to the South Devon Sidings and the left-hand arm on the leg of the gantry routes that way. An underslung centre-pivot arm routes to the Down Main. The signals on top of the gantry route, from the left, as follows: Down Main to Up Southern; Down Main; Platform 3 to Up Southern. Immediately above the cab of the diesel can be seen the signal routing from Platform 3 to Down Main. The large bracket signal in the distance indicates the three-way split of the Up Main into Platforms 4, 5 and 6.

The scene in 1985 shows powerful colour-lights with fibre-optic-fed route indicators. The apparent simplicity disguises the fiendish complication of the circuitry. West box, with 131 levers controlling the junction, has subsequently been preserved in working order at Crewe Heritage Centre.

A similar view looking west from Platform 5 in 1974. The 1 in 36 incline to Exeter Central and Waterloo is on the left, while a Type 3 at Platform 4 awaits the signal and route indicator for 'Branch' or 'Main'; the ground disc at the foot of the post routes to the Up Main. The West signal box dates from 1913, while the building supporting the water tank on the far right might date from 1844. The second photograph shows the old order changing - West box is out of service and being dismantled for preservation.

Turning slightly to our right, we see the complications of Steam Age track layouts, again in 1974. This is the view west from a Barnstaple train waiting at Platform 6. The other lines are goods lines, sidings and connections to the locomotive depot, all essential in the days of heavy freight services, of engine changing, and of shunting engines requiring to take empty coaches from sidings to attach to overloaded trains to permit paying passengers to find a seat. In 1985 the new Exeter Panel Signal Box is beginning to dominate the area.

At the east end of Exeter St David's in 1971, these four stop signals were jointly controlled by Exeter East, behind the camera (his Down Starting signals), and Exeter Middle box, at the far end of the broad/narrow gauge freight transfer shed on the right (his Down Homes). The signals route to the down side of the station; from the left they are: to Down Bay (Platform 2), to Platform 1, to Down Main, and to Platform 3. Below the stop signals are 'Warning/Calling-on' arms and West box's Inner Distant signals.

The equivalent signal in colour-light form viewed from about where the old East box used to be. It signals the five routes through the station, using 'Down' or 'Up' lines indiscriminately to provide the maximum number of routes.

To Ann, for all her deep thinking
and actions on the Dighty Connect
project in Dundee.

Contents

Introduction & About the Authors

This book is a manifesto urging deeper thought about *what* we design, as well as *how* and *why* we design. Whilst this may sound like a criticism of our fellow designers, this is not our intention. As we wrote it, our hearts were filled much more with optimism for the future than criticism for the past. The world we live in presents a myriad of complex, critical challenges which design has the potential to resolve.

Professional designers are not even the primary audience we seek to influence with our manifesto. As design thinking deepens, its reach widens. We would love to think that this work forms a small part of a much bigger movement that turns policymakers, government ministers, company CEOs and other makers-of-big-decisions into deep design thinkers.

When future generations look back and reflect on how we managed to steer away from our climate-warming, species-killing, polluting habits of the past toward a more productive, life-fulfilling and equitable future, our dream is that they might see the hand of deep design thinking on the tiller.

With these as our intentions, we have deliberately kept the book short to try to make it accessible to both designers and non-designers alike.

We are father and son, who have both been Professors of Design and both believe that deeper design thinking will lead to more well-considered design, more deliberate design, more responsible design and more valuable designs.

Seaton launched the first Masters course in Ecological Design in the UK (Robert Gordon University 1993). He led the Natural Design Group at Duncan of Jordanstone College of Art and Design (Dundee University) and the Masters in Ecological Design Thinking at Schumacher College in Devon. He has supervised over 25 PhDs in a variety of design-related subjects. He was professor at Robert Gordon University from 1987 to

1998, at Dundee University from 1999 to 2019 and is now Professor Emeritus at both universities.

Mike worked as a research scientist and a product designer for several years and then was Director of the Design Research Centre at Brunel University. His book, *Product Design: Systematic Methods for the Development of New Products*,[1] was published in 1995 and he went on to be Professor and Dean at Ravensbourne College of Design and Communication from 1996 to 2001. He has been an independent consultant since 2001 and published his latest books, *The Strategy Manual*[2] in 2020 and *Core Values*[3] in 2023.

Mike Baxter and Seaton Baxter, London, 2024

Deep Design Thinking

CHAPTER 1: The Nature of Design

Our journey begins by trying to pin down what design actually is. What, if anything, makes it distinctive? How is it, if indeed it is, different from any other intellectual endeavour or any other professional practice? To do so, we will briefly examine the historical origins of design. Then, in Chapter 2, we will add a layer to consider 'design thinking'. Is design thinking merely the thinking designers do, as they design? Or are there lessons for non-designers to learn from? Is there value to be gained by other professionals thinking like designers do? In which case, what is the nature of that design thinking, what is its value and who should benefit from it?

1.1 When did 'design' begin?

It is often thought that 'design' is a modern phenomenon. The term 'designer' started to appear in popular culture in the 1970s and 1980s (Fig. 1).

When we try to bring famous product designers to mind, we might think of Philippe Starck, Jonathan Ive and James Dyson, who did their most notable work in the 1980s and 90s. Fashion designers such as Cristóbal Balenciaga, Christian Dior, Yves Saint Laurent and Hubert De Givenchy take us back a little further to the 1950s and 60s, although Coco Chanel came to fame in the 1920's. Further back in time, Charles Frederick Worth, in the 1850s, was the first designer to feature his name in the labels of his garments. Further back still, Rose Bertin was the first fashion designer to gain widespread recognition, by virtue of designing clothes for Marie Antionette in the 1770s.

Some design historians, such as John Heskett,[4] consider the origins of design to lie within the Industrial Revolution and the development of mass production in the 1700s and 1800s.

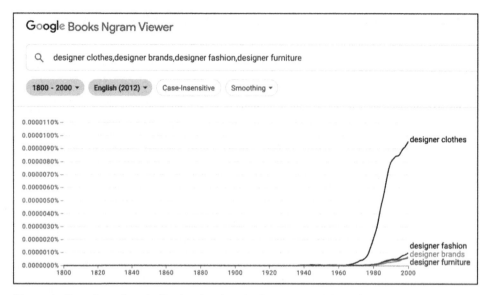

Figure 1. Data from Google Books showing the frequency of the selected words as a percentage of all bigrams (two-word pairings) in the entire Google Books dataset.

But that would overlook some very fine early architectural design. Christopher Wren redesigned St Paul's Cathedral[5] in London starting in 1669. Mimar Sinan designed the Selimiye Mosque[6] in Edirne, Turkey, starting in 1568 and Michelangelo designed the Laurentian Library in Florence, starting in 1523. The title of 'first ever architect' is often bestowed upon Imhotep, who designed the Step Pyramid of Djoser,[7] 27 centuries BCE.

All of which led Victor Margolin[8] to suggest that *"rather than considering design to be a product of industrialisation, we need to think more broadly about the conception and planning of material and visual culture. This enables us to find design in all cultures while at the same time comparing the different conceptions of design and the ways of organising design practice"*.

He went on to propose *"moving back in time to the beginnings of human culture, we can start with Southern African rock paintings as early forms of social communication and then show how such communication continued with the development of pictographs and alphabets. We can also consider African wood carvers who produced headrests, weapons and other material goods as designers within their own cultures at particular historical moments"*. Margolin seems to be positioning the origin of design at the start of creative endeavours by modern humans, perhaps around 30 or 40,000 years ago.

Were we, however, the first creative creatures to 'design'? Chimpanzees in the wild have been observed to manufacture and use a wide variety of tools. Their tools for feeding include hammers, gouges, sponges, hooks, picks, scoops and different long thin sticks, which they use to 'fish' for termites, probe for bees or dip for ants or for honey.[9] One particular population of chimps breaks off branches, sometimes sharpening one end with their teeth, in order to 'spear' bushbabies, hidden in cavities in trees, which they then eat.[10]

So, the origins of designs may now be pushed back a few million years, into the evolutionary history of our primate ancestors.

But there is an even bigger historical issue to grapple with. Very much bigger! To do this requires a quick digression from biology to physics.

Here is what the Simple English version of Wikipedia says about Negentropy:[11]

> *"Negentropy is reverse entropy. It means things becoming more in order. Here 'order' means organisation, structure and function: the opposite of randomness or chaos. One example of negentropy is a star system such as the Solar System. Another example is life.*
>
> *As a general rule, everything in the universe tends towards entropy. Star systems eventually become dead. All energy has gone, and everything in the system is at the temperature of the surrounding space. The opposite of entropy is negentropy. It is a temporary condition in which certain things are hotter and more highly organised than the surrounding space. This is the second law of thermodynamics:*
>
>> *The second law of thermodynamics states that the total entropy of an isolated system always increases over time.*

Life is considered to be negentropic because it converts things which have less order, such as food, into things with more order, such as cells in the body, tissues, and organs. In doing so, it gives off heat. Another example of negentropic things are societies, or social systems, because they take disorderly things such as communications, and make them more orderly and useful."

1.2 What is a design?

Let's, for the moment, stop thinking about 'design' as a verb and just think of the noun. What is a 'design'? Could it be that the very 'order' that all negentropic things display is actually their 'design'?

Solar systems have a heliocentric design. At the centre is a sun. Around it, planets have stable orbits where the sun's gravitational pull is equal to the centrifugal force of the orbiting planet.

Snowflakes come in many different shapes and sizes, but all share a common hexagonal design pattern,[12] derived from the shape of water crystals. *See Note on Design Patterns at the end of this chapter to explore how our use of the term design patterns, here, relates to Christopher Alexander's Design Patterns.*

Living things are categorised and labelled on the basis of their design patterns and how these patterns differ from similar species. Botanists use floral formulae to describe the design patterns of flowers of different species. So, for example, the Scarlet Pimpernel *(Anagallis arvensis)* has the floral formula K5 [C(5) A5] G(5), which indicates that it has 5 free sepals, 5 petals joined to its 5 stamens and a pistil formed of 5 fused carpels.

So, 'designs' are a feature of our entire universe. Wherever order emerges from the background of chaos, the pattern of orderliness can be thought of as a 'design', especially when that pattern is repeated across multiple instances of similar orderliness (e.g. solar systems, snowflakes and organic life-forms). This is not to suggest that these designs are the product of any intentional design process, nor that they require the existence of a designer. The 'design' of a solar system can be explained best by the physics of forces that move objects of large mass. The 'design' of snowflakes is best explained by the physical chemistry of water crystals. The design of living things is best explained by evolution through natural selection.

Here's how Adrian Bejan[13] reflects on 'designs':

> "… designs are everywhere, around us and inside us. The most obvious and best known are the tree-shaped designs, the arborescent flow structures of river basins, human lungs, lightening, vascular tissue, urban traffic, snowflakes, river deltas, global air traffic and vegetation [… another] class is the round cross section of ducts, and they cover the board from blood vessels, pulmonary airways, and earthworm galleries to the 'pipes' carved by rain water in wet soil and the hill slopes of the smallest rivulets of the river basin. Technologies of many kinds employ round ducts, and for good reason: they offer greater access to what flows, greater than in the absence of round cross sections.

> Less known are the rhythms of nature, the designs that represent organization in time, not in space. In most places, the flows that sweep areas and volumes flow in two distinct ways. In the river basin, the water first flows as seepage in the hill slopes (by diffusion called Darcy flow), and later as streams in river channels. This combination is the physics of what others call 'anomalous diffusion'. The first way is slow and short distance, whilst the second is fast and long-distance. Mysteriously, it seems, the water spends roughly the same amount of time by flowing slowly (as seepage) and by flowing fast (as channel flow). The equality of time is the rhythm, and it is predictable from physics."

So, let us acknowledge, and celebrate, the continuum of designs that make up our world, ranging from solar systems and snowflakes at one end to Air Jordans and Philippe Starck's lemon squeezer at the other end (Fig. 2).

Identifying what all the designs in this continuum have in common gives a definition of all designs: an arrangement of orderliness (a pattern) with consistent structural, organisational or functional features (a design).

Figure 2. A Continuum of Designs

A Note on Design Patterns

It is worth noting, at this point, that our discussion, above, is not how most designers would discuss design patterns. We have been using the term 'design pattern' to mean an arrangement of negentropic orderliness, such as a solar system or a snowflake. Whilst this is a valid literal use of the term – as we've just defined – an arrangement of orderliness (a pattern) with consistent structural, organisational or functional features (a design), a designer would see a design pattern in a much more process-oriented perspective. They would say a design pattern "describes a problem which occurs over and over again in our environment, and then describes the core of the solution to that problem, in such a way that you can use this solution a million times over, without ever doing it the same way twice."[14]

First applied to architecture, a design pattern, for example, for a building's main entranceway would require it to be positioned 'where it can be seen immediately from the main avenues of approach and give it a bold, visible shape.' This, according to the founding father of architectural design patterns, Christopher Alexander, produces timeless ways of building because it defines only the essential repeatable aspects of design and not the size, style or construction by which the design pattern is applied.

This design patterns approach has been applied[15] to fields as diverse as garden design and software engineering.

CHAPTER 2: Design Thinking

Let's begin with a thought experiment. Imagine you are a dextrous, visually capable primate and that you are trying to break open a nut with a stone. With one huge swing you miss the nut completely but break a flake off the stone you were using as a hammer. The flake is sharp and useful for cutting. You have just produced a rudimentary knife.

If we imagine the process of design to have two component parts – design-doing and design-thinking – what just happened definitely qualifies as design-doing. You undertook an action that resulted in a design – the design of a rudimentary knife, well suited to the purpose you attribute to it – cutting – because it has a sharp 'blade'.

So, did you just 'design' a rudimentary knife? Probably not, because an essential part of design thinking is intentionality.

The late Daniel Dennett has a phrase, which he'd probably have used if we'd told him our knife-designing thought experiment. It is 'competence without comprehension' and he has this image to illustrate it (Fig. 3).

Here is how Dennett explains competence without comprehension:[16]

> "On the left is an Australian termite castle, on the right is Sagrada Familia – remarkably similar in overall shape and structure and materials etc. But the processes by which these two structures have been created is fundamentally different – the termite castle is built by millions of clueless termites – there is no boss termite, no architect termite, no contractors, or subcontractors, just millions of termites doing their own mindless tasks and amazingly the termite castle with many outstanding design features emerges from their very competent but clueless behaviour. The Sagrada Familia, on the other hand, is the result of an archetypal, charismatic, mad, genius hero. The top-down king of design, who had blueprints, manifestos and proof of concepts and it was all planned out in advance. Architect and artist Gaudi lorded it over his people, who in turn lorded it over their people who in turn lorded it over the stonecutters and builders.

We don't live in a mind-first universe, we live in a matter-first universe and the invention of 'mind' was a very recent invention on this planet. Termites are not intelligent designers; beavers are not intelligent designers. We are the first truly intelligent designers and we came along very late in the evolutionary tree of life."

The key to what Dennett calls "intelligent design" is purpose or intention. Gaudi intended Sagrada Familia to look and function as it does. The termites didn't.

Figure 3. A termite mound and the Sagrada Familia illustrating Daniel Dennett's principle of competence without comprehension (Image sources: Termite mound, Cape York Peninsula © Fiona Stewart, Queensland, Australia. Sagrada Familia, Barcelona by C messier, CC BY-SA 4.0, via Wikimedia Commons)

Alëna Iouguina[17] used a quote from Michelangelo to expand on the notion of intentionality in design:

"In every block of marble I see a statue as plain as though it stood before me, shaped and perfect in attitude and in action. I have only to hew away the rough walls that imprison the lovely apparition to reveal it to the other eyes as mine see it."

Iouguina then went on to cite Proffitt et al's[18] discovery that capuchin monkeys in Brazil deliberately break stones to produce sharp-edged flakes, similar to early hominid tools. The key question, however, is whether they did it with the same intentionality as early humans. Did they 'see' the tool 'inside' the rock before they set about making it?

To try to date the origins of intentional design, Patrick Schmidt[19] explored a variety of early human endeavours and argued that three such endeavours provided strong indications of intentionality:

1. The heat treatment of stone to improve its quality for tool knapping;
2. The reddening of yellow ochre with fire;
3. The distillation of plant exudations to produce glues.

These, Schmidt argued, provide particularly strong evidence on intentionality because they do not involve immediately visible transformations of the shapes of objects. Not able to be guided by the progressive changes in shape of the things they were creating, they must, presumably, have had their intention in their mind as they worked towards it. Artefacts indicating the use of these techniques appear around 200,000 years ago in Neanderthal populations and 100,000 years ago in Homo sapiens. Since these dates don't correlate with either the appearance of those species, nor their migration to new environments, Schmidt takes the appearance of these technologies to be indicative of a particular turning point in evolution – the origin of intentional design.

Whilst convenient to have such a start date for intentional design, it seems likely that the origins of intentionality are far from finally resolved. Especially when a new candidate has entered the race to be the earliest intentional designer. It is … wait for it … the humble octopus![20] More specifically, the Veined Octopus, *Amphioctopus marginatus* from Indonesia, several of whom have been observed[21] moving awkwardly with a stilted gait because they are carrying a pair of coconut shells between their legs, just in case they need them to hide inside in the event of a predator attack.

2.1 The different processes by which designs are produced

If, as suggested above, a 'design' is 'an arrangement of orderliness' that stands out from the background state of chaos in the universe, it must be as a result of some order-producing force. Most of these order-producing forces are non-purposeful. They are not intentionally designed (see the left side of Fig. 4). Solar systems and snowflakes are products of the forces of physics and the forces of chemistry, respectively. Equally, sunflowers and squirrels weren't intentionally designed. Yet, unlike solar systems and snowflakes, they didn't simply appear in their present form as the product of a law of physics or chemistry. They came about through an iterative process of millions of gradually evolving designs, each adapted to the ecological niche of their era, until they turned into the designs we recognise today. This is shown as the separation of non-iterative and iterative processes in the left side of Figure 4.

It was only when this same evolutionary process gave rise to big-brained animals (primates, octopi etc.) that the capacity for intentional design arrived (see the right side of Fig. 4). Big brains can hold a purpose in mind long enough for solutions to be designed to achieve that purpose. Sticks can be fashioned to fish for termites, rocks can be chipped away to produce a hand axe, horse-drawn carriages can be motorised to dispense with the need for the horse and sports shoes can be designed and marketed with a baseball star's name to make lots and lots of money (over $6.5 billion in 2023 for Nike's Jordan brand).[22] This is the iterative, purposeful process we call design thinking.

The final branch of the right side of Figure 4 is a purposeful but non-iterative design process. Does this even exist? Is such a thing possible? One particular design seems to stand out as an emblematic example of this unusual design process.

One Monday morning in September 1984, Professor Alec Jeffreys[23] was studying some x-ray results in his genetics lab at Leicester University. With the relatively primitive equipment available to him at the time, he

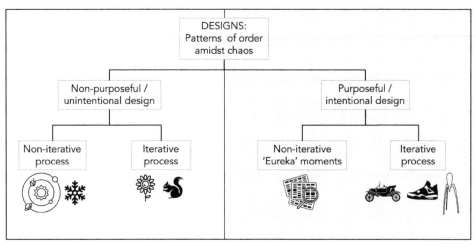

Figure 4. A taxonomy of processes for producing 'designs'

was trying to understand the basic mechanisms of genetic inheritance in humans and his x-rays results were part of a lengthy process to try to identify individual genes, deduce their function and explore their inheritance. He had taken samples from several family members of his lab technician and after a few moments of looking at the x-ray results of their genes, Jeffreys had what he described as a 'eureka' moment. There were clear patterns of both similarity and difference in the genetic results of the different family members. Within half an hour he began to realise the potential applications for his discovery, in both forensics (DNA fingerprinting) and in proving family relationships in immigration disputes. The 'design' of DNA profiling seems to be an example of purposeful but non-iterative design processes. Jeffreys was clearly engaged in the most purposeful behaviour: he was seeking to identify, within strands of DNA, the genes that underpin inherited traits in humans. As an offshoot of that intentional work he, by accident, discovered a design (in this case the design of a service) for producing a genetic 'fingerprint' that could be used to identify individuals and compare the relatedness of pairs of individuals. Being purposefully or intentionally involved in one activity and unintentionally producing a design as an offshoot of that activity seems to describe a great many 'Eureka' moments and hence gives rise to a non-iterative yet still purposeful way that humans design.

2.2 Design creativity

The ability to 'see the tool inside the rock' before making it marked the onset of what we now consider to be intentional design. This also marked the start of design thinking as opposed to simply 'design doing' *(see Note below on Differentiating Designing from Design Thinking)* where:

- a design was found and used (e.g. a stone that could serve as a hammer to crack a nut);
- a design was produced by accident (e.g. cracking off a sharp flake from a stone being used as a hammer and discovering it could be used as a rudimentary knife).

Once design thinking began, it wouldn't take long for these early designers to realise they weren't limited to seeing just one tool inside the rock; they could visualise several alternative tools and try to work out, in their heads, which would work best (Fig. 5). To be able to work this out, they would need to be clear about what the tool was for. A fine slender arrowhead might be better for hunting small prey, whereas a bigger heavier arrowhead might be needed for large prey.

As they get more ambitious with their designs, so their design thinking evolves and soon they are deliberately setting out to think of all possible design ideas to achieve their purpose and then combining and synthesising the best ideas that they will then make.

Design thinking, therefore, has two defining features, so far:

1. A clear purpose that the design solution needs to serve.
2. A creative process to come up with design ideas to serve this intended purpose.

These two features of design thinking would have had a profound impact on human evolution. What was previously an arduous and hugely time-consuming process of trial-and-error making was now turned into purposeful design thinking, a much faster and more efficient process that didn't necessarily require any making until all the design decisions have been made. This, combined with the cultural transmission of ideas across generations, was probably what brought about Homo sapiens' "Great Leap Forward"[24] into behavioural modernity.

Figure 5. Seeing the tool inside the rock will soon be followed by thinking of alternative designs for different purposes (Image from Midjourney)

A Note on Differentiating Designing from Design Thinking

Throughout this book, we place a lot of emphasis on 'design thinking'. This comes from wanting to emphasise the intentionality that design thinking introduces into a world full of unintentional designs. What we don't want to infer from this is that all designing happens in the mind of the designer. Making, in some form or another, manifests the design solution for a consumer, user, viewer, listener or reader to interact with. It is this interaction, if successful, that will produce the intended outcome of the design. Making, especially for designer-makers, also forms a key part of the process of designing. It is through making that progress towards the design solution is achieved.

Indeed, Adrian Forty[25] argues that it was Wedgwood's drive to scale up pottery manufacturing and standardise its product range in the late 1700's that first separated design from production.

> "*The operation of designing thus became not just separate but also geographically removed from the manufacture of the pots.*"

Design and making were, according to Forty's logic, much more of an integral process prior to this.

So, why our emphasis on design thinking? Well, firstly, we believe that design thinking is where most of the value is added to most of the things that are designed. In nearly all the design processes we have worked on, witnessed or studied, sketching and prototyping have been an important part of the process but mostly to enable design thinking to progress. Perhaps most importantly, our message from this entire book is that design ought to be deeper; it ought to solve bigger problems; it ought to aspire to grander solutions. The only way it is going to do this is by *thinking* more deeply about what it is we design and how we design.

The nature of the creative process underpinning intentional design has been studied for several decades. J P Guilford, one of the founders of the psychology of creativity,[26] was the first to point out, in 1956, that creativity comes about by means of divergent thinking followed by convergent thinking.

Divergent thinking (from the word diverge, meaning to move apart) is the ability to think of lots of ideas. Guilford identified four key characteristics of divergent thinking:[27]

1. *Fluency* - the ability to produce a great number of ideas in a short period of time;
2. *Flexibility* - the ability to simultaneously propose a variety of approaches to your design challenge;
3. *Originality* - the ability to produce new, original ideas;
4. *Elaboration* - the ability to systematise, organise and further develop the details of an idea in your head.

Convergent thinking (from the word converge, meaning moving closer together) is often thought of as simply selecting the best or the correct idea produced during divergent thinking. This, however, is an over-simplification. Part of convergent thinking, as the name suggests, is the bringing together, the combining, the hybridisation or the synthesis of multiple individual ideas - this is creative convergence and is much more creative than simply idea selection.

What injects creativity into design is, therefore, a combination of divergent and convergent thinking. Think of a wide range of design possibilities and then merge, combine and synthesise them until you have a coherent solution to whatever challenge your design is responding to.

Bounded creativity. From what has just been said, you might imagine that the aim of divergent thinking is to produce lots and lots of ideas. Whilst the volume of ideas is important, this is not the only thing that is important. Divergent thinking requires you to think of lots of ideas *matching a given set of criteria*. This is not just creativity. It's bounded creativity[28] and that's a lot harder. A substantial body of research has shown that bounded creativity follows the Goldilocks principle:[29] creativity is boosted by some constraints but hampered by too many constraints.

Design is, therefore, an iterative cycle of setting constraints, thinking of lots of ideas matching those constraints, converging on the best ideas and then re-evaluating, refining the constraints and repeating the divergent / convergent thinking process.

2.3 Iterative processes in design thinking

The next step towards modern design thinking may have taken a great deal longer to come about because it only becomes necessary as the things we design become a lot more complex.

As an example, let's imagine a medieval designer being asked to design a plough (by 1000 CE most of the elements of a modern plough have been invented). This is no simple matter of 'seeing the tool in the rock' before starting to make it. It's just too complicated. Too many parts, each performing specialist tasks.

What our medieval designer needs to realise is that you don't need to get from ideation to realisation in a single leap. Instead design thinking can happen iteratively in stages.

Our designer's first stage could specify what this particular plough is for and what functions it needs to perform. Is it merely for scratching the surface of the soil (as the earliest ploughs did)? Or does it need to slice through the soil so seeds can be planted at depth and, if so, what depth? Or does it need to turn the soil over, to bury and compost the surface vegetation?

To maximise the creativity of this stage, we should think divergently– what are all the possible types of ploughs we could design and what are all the different functions they could perform? Then we think convergently - what is the best possible type of plough or what is the best combination of functions for our present purposes?

The second stage starts to identify the plough's component parts and how they contribute to the plough's overall purpose. This remains highly conceptual, at this stage. We don't need to know what materials the components will be made of, nor how they will be made. We only need to know the key characteristics that will deliver that component's functionality. Our medieval designer identifies four key elements for his plough:

1. A beam to apply the force of a draft animal to the plough,
2. A cutter to cut the turf ahead of the plough,
3. A ploughshare to dig through the soil at a particular depth and
4. A mouldboard attached to one side of the ploughshare to turn the soil over.

Again, we go through divergent and convergent thinking, to consider all possible concepts and then narrow down to a single, fit-for-purpose concept for our plough.

The third and final stage is design-for-making. Here is where our designer needs to decide on materials, and methods of production and construction. All possible embodiments of our plough should be considered and then these divergent ideas should be converged to the one final design we are going to make.

This is a lot of thinking, a lot of deciding and a lot of remembering to do if it is all done in the designer's head. Except, of course, it doesn't have to be …

2.4 Design sketching and prototyping

The final attribute of modern design thinking is the external storage of design ideas, which is vital for working on complex designs. Design thinking doesn't have to remain as thoughts inside the designer's head. Design ideas can be sketched, they can be modelled and prototyped, and of course, tried out and tested. Indeed, sketching and prototyping continue to be considered as foundational skills for many design professions.

Sketching can also do a lot more than passively store the ideas in a designer's head. The act of sketching can reframe design thinking and lead to new design ideas. Sketches can also be shared, enabling group input into the design process.

Design prototypes are representations of one or more aspects of a design that are amenable to testing or evaluation, in some way. These prototypes could be digital or physical (e.g. card, foam board, 3d printed or a 'toile' in fashion design). They can be used to test form or function and such tests can be deployed just within the design team (Is this what we thought it would do / look like?), with a client, retailer, purchaser or user (Is this what you wanted? Does it work as expected? Would you buy such a design if it was available at a particular price?).

Whilst sketches and prototypes can be an integral part of the designer's workflow throughout the design process, they also constitute key milestones demarcating distinct design stages. Let's explore this through the work of Leonardo da Vinci, the master sketcher.

Da Vinci studied the flight of birds and the design of flying machines for over 20 years. In that time, he produced over 500 sketches and wrote thirty-five thousand words on the subject. He soon disputed Aristotle's belief that birds floated on air like ships on water and some of his early work shows him wrestling with the idea of a heavier-than-air bird overcoming the forces of gravity (yes, he had a rudimentary understanding of gravity a century before Isaac Newton's apple fell from a tree). Some of his sketches are trying to work out where the centre of gravity of a bird is (or any other flying object) – they show him tussling with the fundamental principles of flight. Then he moves on to sketching the key ingredients for flight, like wings (both of birds and of man-made wings). In doing so, he discovered that the upper surface of a bird's wing is more convex than the lower surface, giving rise to air-pressure differences and aerodynamic lift. He then sketched the mechanics of flight. For birds he examined how they flapped their wings to take off, steer their flight and land again. For human powered flight he sketched lever-mechanisms to convert arm and leg muscle power into wing movement. All of which led to his famous sketches of entire flying machines most notable of which are his ornithopter and helical blade helicopter.

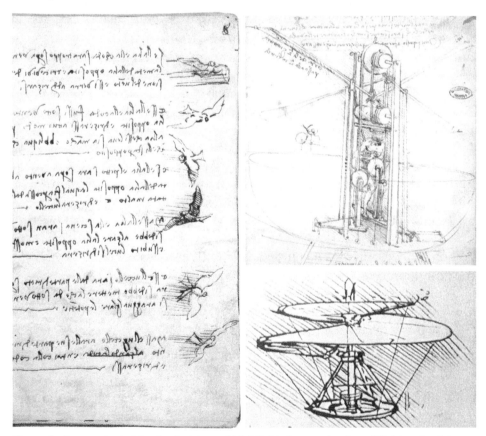

Figure 6. Leonardo da Vinci's sketches of bird flight, the mechanics of flight and a flying machine (all from Wikipedia)

Da Vinci's sketches[30] (Fig. 6) show intentionality, creative thinking and iterative steps in the pursuit of a design solution:

1. The idea of flight, studied in birds;
2. The core principles of flight (aerodynamic lift and centre of gravity), explored both experimentally and by observing bird-flight;
3. The component mechanisms needed for flight (wings and power-transfer mechanisms);
4. A complete design for a flying machine.

This transforms design from a single step process to a multi-stage iterative process. For complex designs, this is another big leap forward. As the design evolves it can be 'instantiated' or 'exemplified' – it can be realised in a single sketch or prototype, which can then be tested for fitness-for-purpose. So, designs can be created iteratively, by successive approximation, with validation steps between each iteration.

2.5 The design thinking process: a synthesis

The multi-stage iterative nature of design thinking has been recognised in different ways in the published design literature (the examples in Fig. 7 are from the Design Council[31] and from Mike Baxter[32]).

Although they differ in the number of iterative stages contained within the design process, they share:

1. A sequence of stages that are iterative and progressively move towards a design solution.
2. Each stage comprises divergent thinking followed by convergent thinking.
3. Each stage produces an instance of the design that can be tested for its fitness-for-purpose.

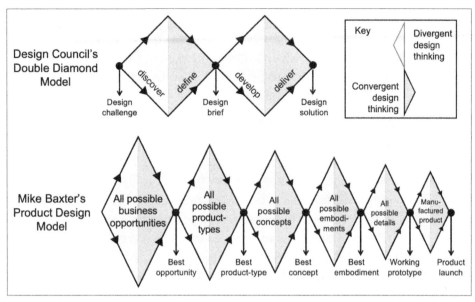

Figure 7. Models of the Design Thinking Process

The complete **design thinking** process can be defined, in full, as follows:

1. Design is intentional or purposeful and, therefore, **the design thinking process begins by defining its intended outcome.** Often, this outcome will be defined in terms of a challenge that the user, client or customer seeks to overcome. This challenge could be solving a problem or exploiting an opportunity. In different fields of design, the challenge could be functional (enabling a user to perform some function) or communicative (communicating a message or articulating a style). Typically, the outcome sought from a design is specified in a design brief, something many designers consider an essential part of the design process.

2. Design thinking in pursuit of this outcome has four key characteristics:

   a. **The design thinking process is creative-by-nature.** This involves a cycle of:

      i. divergent thinking, which tries to imagine all possible ideas by which a bounded creative challenge could be met, and

ii. convergent thinking, which involves creatively selecting, combining, hybridising and synthesising the ideas created in divergent thinking to find the best solutions to the given bounded, creative challenge.

b. **The design thinking process is iterative and progressively more narrowly focused.** This involves repeated cycles of the divergent / convergent thinking process, but on each iteration, the bounded creative challenge has narrowed compared to the preceding cycle. So, concept design seeks to tackle a broad creative challenge – how in principle could we realise the aspirations set out in the design brief? - but after a preferred concept has been selected, embodiment design seeks to tackle a narrower creative challenge – what are all the ways we could prototype a product or service that realises the aspirations set out in the design brief?

c. **The design thinking produces outputs that can be used to test the fitness-for-purpose of the design it has created.** Design thinking always produces an output at the end of its process (the design). The ultimate test of any design is whether it serves the purpose for which it was designed; does it deliver its intended outcome? In addition, design thinking typically produces an output at the end of each iteration of the design thinking process. This is used to check that progress towards fitness-for-purpose is being maintained and that drift, out-of-scope of the original design brief, is being avoided.

d. **The design thinking process is often non-linear.** Sometimes you will come up with a concept you think matches the design brief perfectly, until you move on to embodiment design and you can't make it work. So, you loop back to concept design and come up with a different concept. Occasionally, you might also loop forward – is the concept I've just come up with likely to be manufacturable for roughly the right price? So, whilst the design thinking process, overall, can be seen as iterative and progressively more narrowly focused, the sequence of steps in that process is not simply sequential.

2.6 The value of design thinking

"There is no area of contemporary life where design – the plan, project, or working hypothesis which constitutes the 'intention' in intentional operations – is not a significant factor in shaping human experience."
Richard Buchanan[33]

Within the logic of the narrative we've just worked through, it is design thinking that brings intentionality into the creation of designs. It is 'seeing the tool inside the rock', before starting to chip away at the stone. At its simplest, therefore, design thinking is the thinking that designers do.

Starting in the 2000s a stream of books and articles began to position design thinking in a very different light. According to Tim Brown,[34] one of the pioneers of this new 'design thinking' movement, all manner of business professionals can think like a designer and transform the way they develop products, services, processes—and even strategy. This promised the value of design without all the inconvenience of having to become, or to hire, a professional designer.

This is an extension of Victor Papanek's suggestion that everyone is a designer.[35] He believed that to design was simply to give expression to a fundamental aspect of human nature – life's creative exploration of novelty. Whilst Brown and others in the new design thinking movement wouldn't necessarily have disagreed, they thought it wasn't that simple.

Roger Martin, who worked together with Tim Brown on consultancy projects and who published his book on design thinking[36] around the same time as Tim Brown, makes an even broader claim. He suggests design thinking should be used to design entire businesses, not just their products and services.

"Innovation has become the holy grail of modern organizational life. The vast majority of organizations, whether for-profit or not, big or small, are frustrated by the slow pace and low level of innovation to which they find themselves limited. [...] in order to overcome this limitation, organizations need to incorporate the best of design thinking into their ways of working

[in order to] counter-balance analytical thinking with intuitive thinking to enable it to both exploit existing knowledge and explore to create new knowledge. [Design thinking helps] organizations design their business to achieve a consistently higher level of innovation and creativity."
Roger Martin

Nobel prize-winner, Herbert Simon,[37] takes us one step further. He suggests that modern humanity is engaged in two great intellectual endeavours:

1. 'Natural sciences', such as physics, chemistry and biology, which set out to understand naturally occurring phenomena and

2. 'Sciences of the artificial', such as engineering, medicine, business and architecture, which sets out to understand artefacts. The 'sciences of the artificial', he went on to suggest are "not with how things are but with how they might be - in short, with design."

Here's how he introduced his thinking in his classic book, *The Sciences of the Artificial:*[38]

"Historically and traditionally, it has been the task of the science disciplines to teach about natural things: how they are and how they work. It has been the task of engineering schools to teach about artificial things: how to make artifacts that have desired properties and how to design.

Engineers are not the only professional designers. Everyone designs who devises courses of action aimed at changing existing situations into preferred ones. The intellectual activity that produces material artifacts is no different fundamentally from the one that prescribes remedies for a sick patient or the one that devises a new sales plan for a company or a social welfare policy for a state. Design, so construed, is the core of all professional training; it is the principal mark that distinguishes the professions from the sciences. Schools of engineering, as well as schools of architecture, business, education, law, and medicine, are all centrally concerned with the process of design."

CHAPTER 3: Deep Thinking

Having established what design and design thinking are, we now begin our journey of exploration of deep design thinking. We'll begin with the concept of '*deep*'; there is surprising depth of meaning in this alone! Having identified the key meanings of the word deep, we will then review how these different meanings help us understand the notion of '*deep thinking*'. We will then investigate how the idea(s) of deep thinking have been applied to specific domains of knowledge (deep learning and deep ecology).

The concept of depth most commonly relates to distance. How deep we are in the ocean or in a gorge is a measure of distance from the surface. How deep we are in a forest is a measure of distance from its edge.

More metaphorical uses of the word deep usually *allude* to a measure of distance. A deep conversation is some distance from everyday conversation or from common-sense understanding. To be deeply immersed in a book is to be some distance from normal awareness of your surroundings. A deep sleep is one that is profound, unbroken and far from wakefulness.

Since deep often refers to vertical distance, deep can refer to low-ness, even when the low-ness is nothing to do with physical distance – a deep voice is a low voice. A deep freezer keeps its contents at a low temperature.

There is also a sense of deep meaning profound, hard to comprehend, difficult to learn and enabling great insight. These meanings probably derive from penetrating deeply (i.e. some considerable distance) into a subject. Deep insight, deep mathematical problems, deep dark secrets.

Finally, there is also a sense in which deep can mean passing through layers or boundaries – deep ice cores[39] – 3,200m of core can travel through deposits reaching back 800,000 years. Deep space means not only passing through the Earth's atmosphere but also beyond the edges of the solar system.

Given that we have just found three senses of the word deep – distance, profound-ness and layered-ness – let's now explore how these apply to deep thinking.

Distance

Deep thinking is clearly some distance beyond superficial thinking. Ask one person in the street about the food they eat and they may say they have no interest in the subject, that they meet their nutritional needs in the most utilitarian way possible and think as little about the subject as possible. Ask the person standing next to them and they might describe the cookery lessons they have taken, the countries they've visited to try different foods, the cookery books they've read, the restaurants they love, the food critics they prefer, the specialist food shops they buy from and how they and their partner experiment with new recipes every Friday night. Clearly, there is considerable distance between the depth of thinking these two people have undertaken.

Profound-ness

Deep thinking is also difficult, profound, insightful yet hard for others to comprehend, compared to shallower thinking. Ask a layman about the mathematical constant Pi and they might say it is approximately 3.14 and is used to work out the area and circumference of circles. Ask a mathematician (or Wikipedia![40]) about Pi and they will explain that it is an *irrational number*, meaning that it cannot be written as the ratio of two integers (although 22/7 and 355/13 are used to approximate it). It is also a *transcendental number*, which means that it is not the solution of any non-constant polynomial equation with rational coefficients. It is also a *continued fraction* because it (like all numbers) can be represented by an infinite series of nested fractions.

Layered-ness

When most of us read a book, we end up deciding if we liked it or not. If we were immersed in reading it, empathised with the characters and were gripped by the plot, we probably liked it. For a literary critic, the evaluation of a book is much more layered and might take in Structuralist, Marxist, Feminist or Psycho-analytic perspectives.

- Structural analysis of the whole book. Does the plot follow a universal story arc? Do the lead characters fit classic protagonist vs antagonist roles? Are the narrative patterns, dialogue and writing style typical of its genre?
- Marxist analysis of the plot. What does the book say about the relationship between its characters and the society they live in? Is there opportunity or oppression, equality or exploitation, are they frail or flourishing?
- Feminist analysis of the characters. How are female characters portrayed? Are gender stereotypes reinforced or challenged?
- Psycho-analytic analysis of individual characters. What are the motives behind the characters' actions? What are the root causes of those motives?

3.1 Deep learning

Deep Learning[41] is a subset of machine learning methods based on artificial neural networks. It appears to fit well into the three senses of the word '*deep*' we have just defined – distance, profound-ness and layered-ness.

Firstly, deep learning works by processing data through multiple layers of self-contained transducers. As illustrated in Figure 8,[42] a deep learning system will begin by identifying the salient edges in the images presented to them. These edges will then be combined into simple shapes and then more complex shapes before a visual pattern that uniquely identifies a type of real-world object (such as an elephant) is recognised and labelled.

Secondly, deep learning is profound learning. Google's AlphaGo program beat Lee Sedol,[43] the #2 ranked Go player in the world at that time, in a 4-1 victory. Soon afterwards, Sedol retired[44] from the profession saying that

"Even if I become the number one, there is an entity that cannot be defeated."

Thirdly, deep learning is some considerable distance from human learning in both its capabilities in specific areas of application (Google translates[45] 100 billion words a day into 133 different languages) and its processes (the response that OpenAI's GPT-3 provides to prompts entered by users is shaped by 175 billion parameters in its model[46] – rumours claim that this has been vastly exceeded by GPT-4[47]).

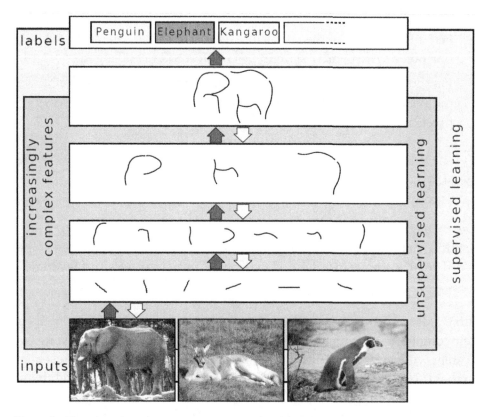

Figure 8. How deep learning systems process visual images using multiple layers of abstraction (Image source: Deep Learning by Sven Behnke, CC BY-SA 4.0, via Wikimedia Commons)

3.2 Deep ecology

The science of ecology was given its name (Ökologie in German) in 1866 by the German scientist Ernst Haeckel. At the time, it was a branch of descriptive natural history that traces its origins back to Herodotus's observation[48] that Nile crocodiles come ashore and lie with their mouths open so sandpipers could step inside, unharmed, to remove leeches.

The first deepening of ecology transformed it from descriptive natural history into analytic biology in the early 1900s. A good example of this is Charles Elton's *Animal Ecology*,[49] first published in 1927. Elton proposed that the science of animal ecology was based on the pyramid structure of feeding relationships within an ecosystem, which could only be understood by researching the behaviour, life history and ecological niche of the individual species within that ecosystem.

Ecology was further deepened by its embrace of mathematical modelling and genetics in the 1950s, and of animal behaviour in the 1960s.

1. **Mathematical modelling**
    Robert MacArthur's famous Warbler paper[50] in 1958, for example, used mathematical modelling to predict how a state of stable equilibrium could allow five warbler species to coexist in the same woods of Vermont and Maine by adopting different specialised feeding strategies.

2. **Genetics**
    Between 1953 and 1955, H.B.D. Kettlewell conducted a series of experiments to investigate genetic variation in the colouring of moths. Several species of European moths, such as the peppered moth (*Biston betularia*) naturally vary from light to dark colouring, a trait that is highly heritable. By means of a series of capture, mark and recapture experiments in woods near Birmingham, Kettlewell showed that predation by birds was:
    a. greater for the lighter moths in a highly polluted, soot-covered woodland environment.

b. greater for the darker moths in a low-pollution, light-coloured lichen-covered woodland.

It was Kettlewell's work that provided clear experimental evidence that natural selection could have a significant effect on genetic variants within a few years rather than the thousands or millions of years that evolutionary change was thought to take.

3. **Animal Behaviour**
    William Hamilton's 1964 paper[51] on kin selection proved how it could be more advantageous for ants, bees and wasps to help their sister (the queen) to reproduce at the expense of reproducing themselves. The key is their peculiar mechanisms of inter-generational gene transfer (haplodiploidy), which means a worker female shares 75% of her sister's genes and only 25% of her own offspring's genes (should she choose to reproduce).

Developments such as these deepened the science of ecology by taking the insights and methods of other scientific disciplines and incorporating them into ecology. So, for example, Kettlewell was one of the first to show that the ecological relationship between individual moths and the level of pollution in their environment was a driver of evolutionary change that was observable over a few generations. This deepened ecology profoundly by crossing what had previously been a discipline boundary between ecology and evolutionary biology. The purpose of ecology – to understand the relationship between organisms and their environment, however, remained unchanged.

When ecology began to serve new purposes, it deepened again. Two examples, at very different scales are gut ecology and the ecology of habitable planets.

Gut Ecology
Inside the human gut lives a microbiological ecosystem, called the microbiome, that is extensive, complex and highly beneficial to its human host. The bacteria in your gut[52] outnumber the cells in the rest of your body by 10-fold and the genes in your gut bacteria outnumber the genes

in the rest of your body by 100-fold. 55% of the dry mass of human faeces is gut bacteria.[53]

The complexity of gut ecology comes partly from the fact the gut comprises two distinct environments for gut bacteria, the stomach and small intestine, that are relatively hostile to gut bacteria due to their secretions (e.g. gastric acid and bile) and hence have fewer bacteria. The colon, on the other hand, has a much higher concentration of bacteria and hundreds of different species.

The complexity of gut ecology also comes from the rich interaction between the gut and its microbiome. During infancy, gut bacteria play a key role in the development of the gut lining (epithelium), making it supportive of friendly gut bacteria and resistant to pathogenic bacteria. Gut bacteria, once established in the gut after the first few years of life, play a key role in the production of antibodies and the regulation of inflammation (via cytokines). Obesity is commonly associated with extensive modification and imbalance of the gut microbiome. Gut bacteria produce vitamins B12 and K, and also produce enzymes that human cells lack for breaking down dietary fibre.[54]

The study of gut ecology is not just a very different type of scientific endeavour compared to Kettlewell's studies of moths in a Birmingham wood, it also deepens what we mean by ecology. Traditional ecology could be defined as the study of plants and animals in the natural world. Gut ecology could be defined as the study of bacteria inside the mammalian gut. A definition of ecology to encompass both disciplines, however, needs to have a higher level of abstraction: the study of any living organism in any environment in which that organism can thrive.

Planetary habitability

"Planetary habitability is a measure of a planet's potential to develop and maintain environments hospitable to life"[55] and research in this area is a particularly challenging application of ecology. This is because speculation is required about the possible environmental conditions under which life could flourish. Whilst most effort is focused on carbon-based life-forms, suggestions have been made that silicon-based life may

be possible; silicon and carbon are in the same group of elements in the periodic table and both are tetravalent (each atom or silicon or carbon can form four bonds with other atoms). Similarly, most effort has concentrated on finding planets with liquid water to support the origin of life, although it is possible that life could be sustained in other solvents, such as ammonia or methane.[56]

By applying ecology to very different types of organisms interacting with very different types of environments, ecological thinking needed to thoroughly re-examine what it took to be its core principles. When Charles Elton wrote Animal Ecology in 1926, he probably didn't give much thought to the application of his insights to silicon life-forms evolving in liquid methane.

The final step to consider in the deepening of ecology is 'Deep Ecology'.

Deep Ecology was created by Professor Arne Naess, a Norwegian philosopher, environmental activist and a mountaineer with affinities to the peace activism of Mahatma Gandhi and the philosophy of Spinoza. Naess's Deep Ecology expanded ecological thinking by embracing new disciplines – philosophy and ethics. It also applied ecology to new purposes – environmentalism.

Naess originated the Deep Ecology Movement in a paper first published in 1973[57] and further developed in association with two American Professors (George Sessions & Bill Devall). His first paper, *"The Shallow and the Deep, Long-Range Ecology Movement"*, contrasts shallow and deep ecology. This provides a foretaste for our approach to the notion of conventional Design Thinking when compared to Deep Design Thinking. At an early stage of the development of Deep Ecology, the authors devised a set of principles which would provide a common platform around which individuals could formulate their own philosophy of Deep Ecology, their "ecosophy." These principles may also be valuable in the formulation of the foundations of Deep Design Thinking and so they are quoted here from the chapter entitled *"Platform Principles of the Deep Ecology Movement"* by Arne Naess and George Sessions in Drengson & Inoue (1995).[58] The eight Platform Principles are:

1. The well-being and flourishing of human and non-human Life on Earth have value in themselves. These values are independent of the usefulness of the non-human world for human purposes.

2. Richness and diversity of life forms contribute to the realisation of these values and are also values in themselves.

3. Humans have no right to reduce this richness and diversity except to satisfy vital needs.

4. The flourishing of human life and cultures is compatible with a substantial decrease of the human population. The flourishing of non-human life requires such a decrease.

5. Present human interference with the non-human world is excessive, and the situation is rapidly worsening.

6. Policies must therefore be changed. These policies affect basic economic, technological and ideological structures. The resulting state of affairs will be deeply different from the present.

7. The ideological change is mainly that of appreciating life quality, rather than adhering to an increasingly higher standard of living. There will be a profound awareness of the difference between big and great.

8. Those who subscribe to the foregoing points have an obligation directly or indirectly to try to implement the necessary changes.

Warwick Fox refers to Naess's formal sense of Deep Ecology, which he says is *"predicated upon the idea of asking progressively deeper questions about the ecological relationships of which we are a part. Naess holds that this deep questioning process ultimately reveals bedrock or end-of-the-line assumptions, which he refers to as fundamentals, and that deep ecological views are derived from such fundamentals while shallow ecological views are not."*[59]

Arne Naess's work on 'deep ecology', might be thought of as the ultimate "ecologically deep thinking." Deep Ecology, as developed by Naess,[60] however, is not a further deepening of the Science of Ecology, it is philosophically expansive rather than scientifically reductive. Naess extended ecology from its roots as an academic discipline and transformed it into a form of political activism.[61]

CHAPTER 4: Deep Design Thinking

In the preceding chapters we have explored the fundamentals of design thinking and of deep thinking. Our challenge, in this chapter, is to somehow fuse these together to discover the defining principles of deep design thinking.

Design thinking is the intentional part of design (seeing the tool inside the rock) and it follows a distinctive process (this is the summary version of the process described in full in Section 2.5):

1. Design is intentional or purposeful and, therefore, the design thinking process begins by defining its intended outcome.

2. Design thinking, in pursuit of this 'intended outcome', has four key characteristics:

    a. The design thinking process is creative-by-nature, involving a cycle of divergent and convergent thinking.

    b. The design thinking process is iterative and progressively more narrowly focused.

    c. The design thinking produces outputs that can be used to test the fitness-for-purpose of the design it has created.

    d. The design thinking process is often non-linear and can loop forwards and backwards.

A great deal of *design thinking* is about setting boundaries and maximising creativity within those boundaries.

A great deal of *deep thinking* is about crossing boundaries and challenging boundaries. We discussed at some length how ecological thinking deepened, firstly by crossing into the disciplines of mathematics, genetics and animal behaviour and secondly by crossing over to very different domains of application. Studying planetary habitability and the gut microbiome are still applications of ecological thinking: they are still about the interactions of organisms and their environment. They are just very different organisms in very different environments.

The case we want to make in this chapter is that the innovative aspect of *deep design thinking* is that it BOTH sets boundaries AND challenges/ crosses boundaries as a core part of its process.

Let's begin with an example, turning again to the humble plough.

The plough has played a key role in the development of human society for the past 10,000 years. Almost half of all habitable land on Earth has been cultivated for agriculture[62] and, in the past 2,000 years, the productivity of that land has more than tripled.[63] By the middle of the 20th century, 140,000 ploughs were being sold every year in the USA alone.[64] There cannot be many 'designs' that have had such a widespread reach (historical and geographical) and such a profound impact on human society.

The story of the plough, however, is not all good news. By turning soil over and burying the ground-cover vegetation, ploughs have a huge impact on soil erosion. The exposed earth is more vulnerable to both water erosion, when it rains, and wind erosion during dry periods. The most dramatic demonstration of this was the dust storms that ravaged the prairies of USA and Canada during the 1930's and removed 75% of the topsoil from the farmland of some regions by 1940.[65] More recently, as agriculture is recognised as a major contributor to carbon emissions, attention has focused on the energy costs of ploughing. Alternative cultivation methods, such as direct drilling, use 75% less energy than ploughing. In addition, different cultivation methods make a big difference to the greenhouse gas emissions from agriculture, although minimising the climate impact of cultivation methods requires striking some delicate balances:[66]

a. ploughing increases the breakdown of organic matter and hence the release of carbon dioxide from the soil;

b. ploughing makes soils more aerobic and hence reduces the release of nitrous oxide, a more potent greenhouse gas that carbon dioxide;

c. fields left unploughed gradually increase their earthworm populations and earthworms aerate the soil, making the soil more aerobic and hence reducing nitrous oxide emissions without ploughing.

So, designing climate-friendly cultivation systems requires a long-term perspective and careful trade-offs between conflicting consequences.

The development of field cultivation systems for agriculture has several of the characteristics of deep design thinking. For most of human history, the design boundaries were clear and firmly set; we need to best cultivate land to maximise crop yields from that land. Over many centuries the design of ploughs improved so that more land could be better cultivated with less human labour. Using draft animals and then tractors accelerated this rate of improvement.

Then, early in the twentieth century, a new system boundary was crossed. Field cultivation systems were no longer just focused on maximising crop yields: they needed to be designed to conserve soil as well. Fast forward to the present day and a new system boundary has been encountered, requiring the agricultural industry to design its way out of being one of the biggest emitters of greenhouse gases in the developed world.

This setting of boundaries to creatively design within, and then crossing boundaries to reset how we design to suit new circumstances, is a key characteristic of deep design thinking. The problem with the plough / agriculture example we've just discussed is that it was an emergent rather than an intentional process. No plough designer foresaw the problems with soil erosion and invented new soil cultivation systems to avoid the dust storms of the 1930s. The disaster happened, with catastrophic consequences. Between 1930 and 1940, 3.5 million people moved out of the worst affected states. It was only after this massive economic and personal hardship had taken place that the need to change the way we cultivated farmland was accepted. Similarly, the climate crisis is upon us and only now are we reframing our design of agricultural systems to reduce their greenhouse gas emissions.

Deep design thinking ought to have, at its heart, the critical hallmark of all design thinking – it should be intentional. We should design our way around anticipated future challenges, not wait for the crises to happen and retrospectively work out what we ought to have done sooner.

4.1 Deep design thinking methods

How can deep design thinking possibly both set boundaries and challenge / cross boundaries as a core part of its process? Surely, there is a fundamental contradiction here. Let's start to unravel it by exploring where design's boundaries come from.

According to many designers, design begins with the design brief.

- *"The design brief is the first part of the design process."*[67]

- *"The design brief is the single most important step in the design process. Without it, you will be lost."*[68]

- *"Every successful design project begins with a design brief."*[69]

- *"A design brief lays out the objectives, goals, and expectations of a design project."*[70]

This, however, begs the question, where does the design brief come from? The UK's Design Council is explicit on this. Their Double Diamond model of the design process (that we saw in Fig. 7) begins with a design challenge – what is the problem or opportunity that gives rise to the need for a novel design solution? With no challenge there is no need to create a design solution and hence no need for a design process. The first diamond in their Double Diamond model takes the design challenge and runs a discovery and definition process around it.

Starting with a design challenge is good, but it still doesn't answer the question "challenging for whom?". The answer, in most design discussions, is the 'user'. Somewhere there is a user who is struggling to do or to experience something they need or desire. Their inability to achieve this need or desire is their challenge. Design then seeks to create a solution by which their need or desire can be attained. Here's how Harvard Business School introduces design thinking:[71]

> *"The essence of design thinking is human-centric and user-specific. It's about the person behind the problem and solution, and requires asking questions such as "Who will be using this product?" and "How will this solution impact the user?"*

To a degree, this is admirable. Much better to identify a 'user', discover their wants and needs and set out to satisfy them, rather than imposing a solution upon them that a designer imagined they might like.

Yet, the design challenge and resulting design brief cannot only be about user needs and wants. Ask a 1930's farmer in the prairie states of America about their needs and wants and it wouldn't have taken them long to mention ploughing. "What's the challenge you're facing?", we might ask. And they'd say scale and efficiency in getting the land cultivated and planted. By 1932, the price of wheat had dropped over 80% compared to 1920,[72] so their most pressing need was to be able to farm bigger areas of land without increasing costs too much. So, bigger ploughs pulled by bigger tractors were designed to meet these needs. Ken Burns' TV series, *The Dust Bowl*[73] shows 10 tractors in a row, each pulling a 30-disc plough, as the commentary describes them working throughout the day and then switching on their lights so they could plough all night as well. The Great Plow-Up, as it came to be known, cultivated 2 million acres of virgin grassland per year in the early 1920's across the Southern Plains of the USA. The challenge of soil erosion, an issue that ended up ruining the lives of millions in the dust-bowl states and causing massive dust pollution as far as Chicago, Boston, New York and Washington DC, would have gone largely unmentioned.

If pressed about soil erosion and the possibility of ploughing risking their topsoil being blown right off their land, our dust bowl farmer might have argued that this was a much bigger issue that they, individually, could do little about. It was, after all, the deliberate policy of the US Government to convert the Great Plains to productive private ownership by means of the Homestead Acts (1862 to 1916).[74] These Acts gave away 10% of the landmass of the USA to 1.6 million homesteaders, on condition that they "improved their plot by cultivating the land".

So, the dust bowl issue arises out of a nested set of (at least) six system layers, each with its own design challenge (Fig. 9).

Avoiding the dust storms of the 1930's would probably have required design challenges to have been resolved at more than one of these system layers.

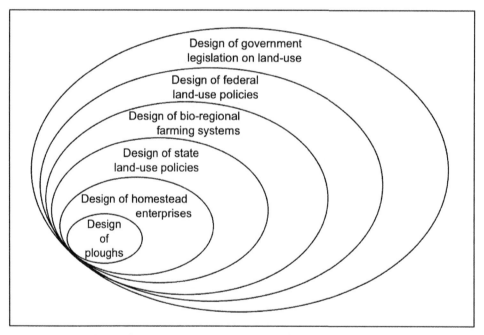

Figure 9. The design challenges at different system layers

4.2 Deep design thinking in practice

Deepening the Design Challenge

So, deep design thinking never takes a design challenge as given. The design challenge, perhaps more than any other input into the design thinking process, needs to be interrogated, analysed and … challenged! Note, by the way, that we are using the term design challenge, not design problem. This is broader. A design challenge could be a problem someone is experiencing that they want to avoid or an opportunity someone sees they want to exploit.

It may be useful, within the lexicon of deep design thinking, to explicitly declare the 'initial design challenge' – what was the challenge that initiated this entire design process? What was the trigger? But then there should be some statement of the 'deepened design challenge'. This ought to deepen thinking about the design challenge in two dimensions. Firstly, point-of-view – for whom is the challenge challenging? A user-centred perspective on this is a great place to start but the design process will often be improved by being informed by other points of view. Whilst the farmer may simply want cultivation efficiency from a plough, an agronomist might warn of the dangers of soil erosion and a US Senator might have questioned the wisdom of requiring the cultivation of the drought-prone Great Plains. We call this the 'stakeholder perspective' on the design challenge and it ought to consider not only who might benefit from the ultimate design solution but also who might be harmed, disadvantaged or inconvenienced by it.

Secondly, the design challenge ought to consider a 'systems perspective'. Can the design challenge be meaningfully defined at higher or lower systems layers. For example, should the design of ploughs have influenced or been influenced by bio-regional land-use policies. There will, of course, often be overlap between the stakeholder and systems perspectives.

Deepening the Design Brief

Having defined a deepened design challenge, this now needs to be translated into a design brief. From a deep design thinking perspective, the brief needs to serve two purposes. It needs to define 'ultimate success criteria' for the design solution. These are the criteria by which we determine if the design solution is good enough to use / launch / publish / mass-produce by evaluating whether it serves the purpose the entire design process was initially set up to serve. These ultimate success criteria are, therefore, fitness-for-purpose thresholds and, ideally, we should also be able to use them to judge the adequacy of the design thinking as the design process progresses. If our design ideas are not heading towards the outcomes we seek, it is better we know early so we can try to find new design ideas or abandon the entire design endeavour.

The second purpose of the design brief is to set the boundaries for the next iterative cycle of the design thinking process ('next-cycle-boundaries'). Remember that the entire creative process depends on creativity being well-bounded. This seeks to place creative endeavours in the 'Goldilocks zone' – not so constrained as to stifle creativity but constrained enough to focus creativity on the design challenge we're trying to resolve. These next-cycle-boundaries may overlap the ultimate success criteria but they will be two distinct sets of success thresholds. Figure 10 shows how deep design thinking moves from design challenge to design brief.

This is an unusual proposition, not commonly found in the design literature. Most design authorities would insist there is a single design brief with a single set of criteria defining the acceptability of a finished design solution. So why are we breaking with convention for deep design thinking? The reason is our firm belief that whilst the ultimate success criteria should remain unchanged throughout the design process, the next-cycle-boundaries change … at every design transition point.

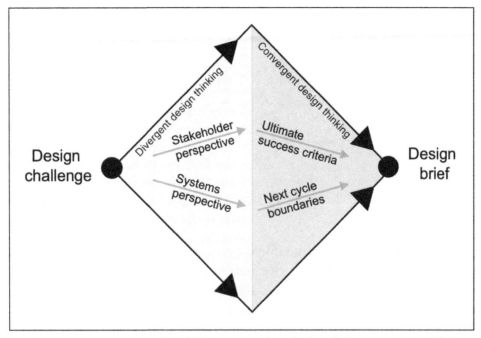

Figure 10. How deep design thinking moves from design challenge to design brief

Deepening Design Transition Points

One of the defining criteria of design thinking is that it progresses through a series of iterative cycles of divergent and convergent thinking, whilst progressively narrowing its focus until a design solution is produced. These iterative cycles are marked by checkpoints or stage-gates, where the design ideas produced so far are tested against the fitness-for-purpose criteria in the design brief (Fig 11).[75] The way this works in practice is that an instance of the design ideas is produced, often in the form of a sketch or a prototype, and it is this instantiation of design thinking that is tested for fitness-for-purpose. If the design is deemed to be acceptable (i.e. it suggests that the design, once complete, will meet the ultimate success criteria and hence resolve the design challenge) then the design process moves on to the next iterative cycle. It is implicit in much writing about the design process that the next-cycle-boundaries will be different from the last-cycle-boundaries, but this is rarely made explicit.

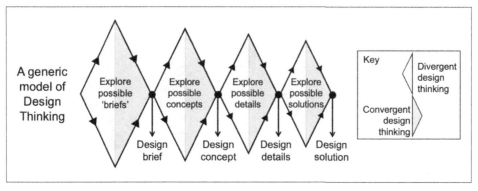

Figure 11. Generic Model of Design Thinking

Here, then, is our deep design thinking perspective on design transition points. The idea of iterative cycles of divergent thinking followed by convergent thinking seems strong. Each of these iterative cycles needs to start with a clear set of creative boundaries and needs to end with an instantiation of the design thinking. We'll delve deeper into the starting point for creative boundaries in a moment but first let's explore why an end point (an 'instantiation of design thinking') is so critical to the design process.

The most common answer is that the design thinking in each iterative cycle needs to be tested against the ultimate success criteria in the design brief to ensure the design process is making progress in the right direction. This, of course, could be done by presenting an array of twenty different design ideas and showing how, between them, they meet the ultimate success criteria. This might be deemed sufficient to permit the design process to progress to the next cycle.

Yet many designers would say this isn't good enough. They would argue that a single best design idea ought to be resolved in whatever level of detail that cycle of the design process requires. This seems to be good practice for two reasons. Firstly, it demands that convergent thinking is pursued to its ultimate conclusion – the convergence of design thinking to a single instance of the design. Secondly, it also acts as a forcing function for the designer or design team. Can they resolve their design thinking to a single instance of design ideas (e.g. a sketch or prototype) that coheres sufficiently to be communicated (here's our best shot so far on how this new design will work and will look like) and evaluated (is it on track to do what we originally wanted it to?).

That's where each iterative cycle needs to end up, but where does it need to start to get there? Clearly, it needs the creative boundaries for divergent and convergent thinking to be set. So, we begin with the design brief. This sets the ultimate success criteria and the next-step-boundaries. We use these next-step-boundaries for the next iteration of divergent thinking and convergent thinking. Let's assume it is a success. We have a coherent single concept for the design solution and, as far as we can determine at this early cycle in the design process, it fits the ultimate-success-criteria. So, we are good to progress on to the next iterative cycle.

Again, let's pause to emphasise that this is not a linear process we're depicting here. If, at the end of one iterative cycle of divergent / convergent thinking, we find we haven't got a single coherent instance of our design thinking that meets the ultimate success criteria, we would need to repeat that cycle. Or if, during our design thinking, we made some quite profound discoveries that reveal our ultimate success criteria are wrong or incomplete, we'd need to go right back to the design challenge, check that it is still valid and re-write the design brief. So, the design process has frequent back-loops to reconcile new discoveries with prior assumptions. It can also have jump-forward loops as well. We might, for example, have come up with a really innovative concept but need to jump forward in the design process to check we have the technology to realise such a design. Once confirmed, we then come back to continue the design process based on that innovative concept.

Whilst the design process is not linear, eventually it must progressively narrow towards a single design solution … it won't be a design process if it doesn't end up with a design! This progressive narrowing is what the next-stage boundaries bring about. By redefining the boundaries for the next stage at each design transition point we ensure the next-stage-boundaries are different from the last-stage-boundaries. Typically, they will narrow. But the non-linearity of the design process demands that they don't always narrow. We might be looping back to re-evaluate our design thinking at a previous stage, in which case they might broaden substantially.

Figure 12 expands the design transition point to show what happens inside it. In the upper part of the black circle an acceptance decision is made about the sketch or prototype produced at the end of the last stage's convergent thinking. The lower part of the circle shows the transition from last-stage boundaries to next-stage boundaries.

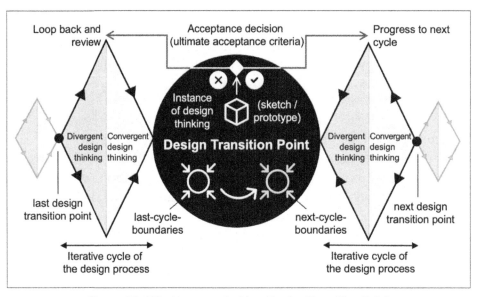

Figure 12. What happens inside a Design Transition Point

Deepening Creative Boundaries

Bearing in mind our previous claim that the innovative aspect of *deep design thinking* is that it BOTH sets boundaries AND challenges / crosses boundaries as a core part of its process, we have now reached the moment of truth. How can it achieve this apparently contradictory feat?

The answer, in the context of Design Transition Points is that we *set* the next-cycle boundaries after our design instance has been deemed acceptable but only after rigorously and creatively *challenging* and seeking to *cross* all the boundaries that have previously constrained our design thinking. This is what makes design thinking deep.

The deep design thinking process would work like this:

1. Like all design processes, we start with a challenge.

2. Unlike some design processes, deep design thinking explicitly sets out to define two distinct sets of criteria in the design brief – 'ultimate success criteria' and 'next-cycle-boundaries'.

3. These two sets of design brief criteria are devised rigorously by firstly exploring in some depth who is 'challenged' by the design challenge (the stakeholder perspective) and secondly by taking a systems view of the challenge and its potential design solution. How different would the challenge look if seen from a higher or lower systems-level perspective?

4. Then, as the design process progresses through its iterative creative cycles, we transition the last-cycle-boundaries into next-cycle-boundaries at each design transition point. This involves repeating the rigorous approach we took in devising the design brief in the first place. Given the progress we have made in developing design ideas, do we need to reframe the design challenge in any way? Does the new design, as it is emerging, affect, for good or for bad, any new stakeholders? Could it impact, again for good or for bad, higher or lower system boundaries in different ways from the ones we envisaged when writing the design brief? Does it look like the emerging design may solve new problems or exploit new opportunities? Could it serve previously unthought-of functions in previously unthought-of situations?

What will have become apparent to any readers who are imagining how deep design thinking might apply to the design process within their organisation is that deep design thinking is disruptive. It doesn't keep the design process nicely contained within its own 'swim-lane'. By challenging and crossing the boundaries set in the original design brief, we may end up working on a totally different project from the one we started with. This will often cross into the swim-lanes of other functions or departments within your organisation. It may also, if this isn't pushing the metaphor too far, result in leaps into whole new swimming pools and possibly even into wide expanses of uncharted ocean!

Yet, isn't this what the world needs more of? Isn't it because designers are kept in their swim-lanes that we have a proliferation of products and services that consumers buy but don't need, use but don't like and replace when they don't have to?

Isn't this deep design thinking approach a better approach to solving the world's problems? Albert Einstein is widely quoted as saying (but almost certainly didn't)[76] that *"if I had an hour to save the world, I would spend 55 minutes defining the problem and 5 minutes solving it"*. The depth of deep design thinking comes mostly from its greater emphasis on defining and continuously re-defining the design problem.

The Making of Deeper Designers

Around the time he was evangelising design thinking to the broader business world, Tim Brown also explained[77] the type of people his global design firm, IDEO, sought to hire:

> *"T-shaped people have two kinds of characteristics, hence the use of the letter "T" to describe them. The vertical stroke of the "T" is a depth of skill that allows them to contribute to the creative process. That can be from any number of different fields: an industrial designer, an architect, a social scientist, a business specialist or a mechanical engineer. The horizontal stroke of the "T" is the disposition for collaboration across disciplines. It is composed of two things. First, empathy. It's important because it allows people to imagine the problem from another perspective- to stand in somebody else's shoes. Second, they tend to get very enthusiastic about other people's disciplines, to the point that they may actually start to practice them. T-shaped people have both depth and breadth in their skills."*

Whilst this resonates with a lot of what is important for deep design thinking, we feel it is missing one vital aspect, which we will explore using Figure 13.

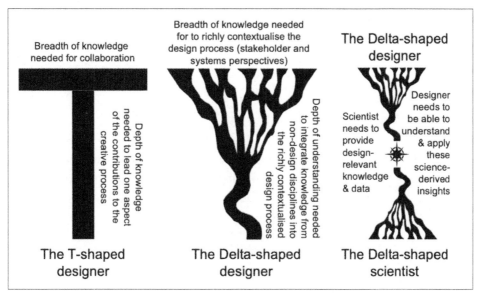

Figure 13. The Delta-Shaped Designer

It may not have been Tim Brown's intention, but his T-shaped designer looks like they apply the depth of their knowledge to one specific aspect of their breadth of knowledge. In a T-shape, depth meets breadth at a single point. This, in our view, sits less well with deep design thinking. Instead, we prefer the idea of a **delta-shaped designer,** where their full breadth of knowledge informs and shapes their area of deep specialism, and the depth of their specialism informs and shapes their full breadth of knowledge.

A delta shaped designer could, for example, be uniquely positioned to integrate their years of experience as an agricultural engineer designing ploughs with recent findings from the atmospheric chemistry of greenhouse gases. Whole new farming enterprises could be designed, with the machinery to both cultivate the land and certify its low-carbon cost.

This is not to suggest that all plough designers need to take a career break to get PhDs in atmospheric chemistry. Rather, they need to find delta-shaped scientists who have the breadth of knowledge to understand how best to apply their depth of expertise to produce design-relevant information. Then the designer needs to deepen their understanding so that they are able to incorporate the science usefully in innovative design thinking.

4.3 The deep design thinking toolkit

The two key points of intervention in the design process to deepen design thinking are the design brief and the design transition points. Our toolkit for doing so couldn't, in principle, be simpler. Deep design thinking adds a 'wrapper' to a conventional design brief.

A conventional design brief defines the user, their challenge(s) and hence the purpose that the new design solution is intended to serve. It will also set out any constraints that the design solution needs to comply with for financial, operational or marketing / sales reasons. Finally, it describes, at a high level, the practicalities of the design process – who needs to do what by when.

The wrapper, that goes around this conventional design brief, will explore a wider range of stakeholders that could be impacted (positively or negatively) by the intended design solution. Will this design solution have any effect on the friends, family, neighbours or colleagues of the user? Who would be involved in the entire lifecycle of this product or service, from extraction of raw materials all the way through to its disposal at end-of-life? If this design solution became widely used, how might people in local areas or regions of its use be affected?

It will also explore how the intended design solution might fit into a variety of systems-level perspectives. Design solutions are intended to have a beneficial effect on their users in one domain of their life but what about other domains? Will it affect their privacy, their security, their comfort or their wealth? Will it affect how they interact with other people? Will it affect how they interact with nature? Will it affect their work-life balance? Will it affect their carbon footprint?

Then, moving away from the user, will our intended design solution affect the market sector in which it will be sold? Could it have a systemic effect on pricing (e.g. price erosion)? Could it start an innovation arms race and, if so, what might be the good and bad consequences of this?

Then beyond the market sector, could our design solution have any global impact? Could it cause pollution? Could it affect biodiversity, wealth inequality, exploitation of labour or depletion of scarce resources?

Imagine writing your conventional design brief on a single side of A4 paper then placing this at the centre of an A3 sheet of paper. This is the deep design brief wrapper. Specific aspects of the conventional design brief can be shown to connect to deeper design implications. In this way, the wrapper defines which boundaries we might choose to challenge and possibly even cross, as the design evolves. It also provides a means to interrogate the conventional design brief. Does it focus on user needs at the expense of any other stakeholder needs? Does it frame the design solution at a single systems level without considering the implications at higher, and possibly lower system levels? Once challenged, and possibly edited in response, the conventional design brief remains the key document guiding design direction-setting and decision-making.

The deep design wrapper is then re-introduced at each design transition point to add depth to the evaluation of the design instance under review. All the questions with which we interrogated the design brief, we now ask again of the sketch or prototype before us.

4.4 Reflections on deep design thinking

Design thinking is a remarkably powerful process on its own. It is an iterative, creative process that progressively narrows to produce a novel solution to a defined challenge. Turning this into deep design thinking requires systems boundaries to be challenged at the transition points between those cycles of iterative creativity. This could be argued to be a relatively modest change to a well-established and widely practised design process. Having taken the time and trouble to write this entire book perhaps gives the game away that we disagree profoundly with this argument. We feel that challenging system boundaries repeatedly within the heart of the design process will not only change what we, as a society, design, but also will transform the impact that our designs will have on our planet, its climate and natural resources and the health and happiness of all the creatures living on it.

In the two chapters that follow we turn to our own individual experiences of deep design thinking in two very different areas of application: strategy design thinking for Mike and ecological design thinking for Seaton. We've written them in auto-biographical form because we both had work to do to establish these as ways of thinking and working. In these chapters we demonstrate how, over our careers, we have written and published several papers and articles setting out why we think strategy design thinking and ecological design thinking ought to be disciplines of professional endeavour, and how we have deepened our own design thinking in the process.

Baxter & Baxter

CHAPTER 5: Mike's Journey - Deep Design Thinking for Strategy

5.1 Strategy as design thinking

For more than a decade, I considered myself a product designer. For the first half of that time, I was working full-time, researching user needs, running usability tests, designing and refining the design of specific products, securing patent protection on those products, negotiating the commercial production of those products and supporting their launch and initial sales promotions. In other words, I was a designer engaged directly in the full design and development lifecycle of my products. In the latter part of that decade, I moved into more of a managerial role, as Director of the Design Research Centre (DRC) at Brunel University. I did some teaching, quite a bit of research into design processes and methods and worked with the fantastic team at the DRC to support their own design and development projects. The culmination of my (and the DRC's) work over this decade was my book *Product Design: A Practical Guide to Systematic Methods of New Product Development*.[78]

Fast forward several years and I had started my own consultancy company. I ended up working with a remarkable range of big global brands (e.g. Avis, Cisco, Dell, Google, HSBC, Lilly, Richemont, Sony PlayStation) on a diverse range of topics, including marketing, sales, analytics and digital transformation. At the same time, I worked as an advisor to a series of start-ups, two of which became the 8th and 9th fastest growing tech start-ups in the UK within a few years of each other (Peerius in 2014 and Ometria in 2018). In the course of all this advisory and consulting work, my interest and role in strategy grew and it quickly became clear that the challenges people encountered in creating great strategies had a lot in common with the challenges of creating great designs.

So, around ten years ago, I decided to focus my consultancy work exclusively on strategy, and alongside my work with clients developing their strategies, I was re-reading all the classic texts on strategy and making sure I kept up to date with new books and papers as they came out.

By the time I felt comfortable that I was up to speed with the published strategy literature, I had become convinced there was a big gap in strategy thinking that needed to be filled. My main conclusion was that most of what had been written on strategy were 'perspectives on strategy'.[79] Michael Porter, like Carl von Clausewitz and Sun Tzu before him, believed that strategy was all about understanding competitors and building defensible barriers to competitive forces. Peter Drucker, and more recently, Steve Blank and Eric Ries, believe strategy is all about understanding and accommodating the needs of customers. And then there are a cluster of strategists who believe strategy is all about organisational capabilities: Frederick Taylor focuses on operational efficiency, Gary Hamel focuses on people and culture, Chan Kim & Renée Mauborgne focus on innovation and Rita Gunther McGrath focuses on managerial agility.

These are all great perspectives on strategy. To a large extent they are all right. But what they missed, in my mind, was how to actually 'do' strategy – strategy-doing like the design-doing we discussed earlier. Where do you start, once you accept that your organisation needs a new strategy? What are the key ingredients and where do you look for the recipe to create that strategy? I started to piece together my own 'workshop manual' on strategy-making.

Although I didn't see it like this at the time, looking back I can see, firstly, a clear trajectory to connect strategy thinking (the way we, professional strategists think about strategy) to design thinking. Secondly, I deepened my strategy thinking in exactly the same way as we've just described for deep design thinking. Here's how I piece together the way my strategy thinking evolved.

In April 2019, I tried to capture the essence of strategy in a four-step process:[80]

1. Strategy is born from the need for priorities – no organisation can do everything;

2. These priorities need to build upon the existing strengths of the organisation;

3. These strengths, once prioritised by strategy, need to be turned into action – a strategy without an action-plan is a wish-list;

4. These actions need to be enabled with the right allocation of resources.

Ultimately, according to my thinking at the time, strategy was all about the amplification of the right organisational strengths by means of prioritisation, action planning and resource-allocation.

That same month, I published *University Strategy 2020*,[81] a research report analysing 52 published strategies of UK Universities. In it, I proposed eight interlinked elements that all good strategies should be designed to contain (see the Strategy Design Model in Figure 14):[82]

1. **Destination** – where are you striving to get to? What is your "winning aspiration?" What is the important end you are striving to reach?

2. **Methods** – what are the handful of core activities that are critical for you to reach your destination? Destination and methods are the essence of strategy. They are what strategy is designed around.

3. **Alignment** – the logic connecting actions to outcomes. If everyone in your organisation is pulling in the same direction, you will achieve more, and achieve it quicker, than if they are pulling in different directions.

4. **Innovation** – the cultivation of new ways of thinking and working. How much innovation does the strategy demand? How will you build the organisational capability and culture to achieve it?

5. **Priority** – the identification of what really matters. Peter Drucker, known as the 'founder of modern management' says *"The worst thing is to do a little bit of everything. It is better to pick the wrong priority than none at all."*[83]

6. **Performance** – data indicative of meaningful progress. "What gets measured, gets managed!" Whilst this may be true, it is not always a good thing if the changes that matter most are the hardest to measure (e.g. aspects of culture change within an organisation). The measurement of progress serves two purposes: firstly, it justifies continued commitment to the strategy and secondly it informs course-correction and fine-tuning of strategy adoption.

7. **Adaptability** – resilience and agility combined. A key element of strategy is defining how the organisation is going to respond to change, how it is going to move fast and take advantage of new opportunities as they arise.

8. **Adoption** – active engagement, willing commitment. The success of every strategy depends on the support it can recruit from the individuals needed to bring about change, which is why we call it adoption: less push, more pull. Putting people at the centre of strategy design ensures their involvement, commitment and active engagement. The governing body and senior leadership need to adopt the strategy and ensure their decisions both support the strategy and avoid eroding or undermining it. Front-line employees and key stakeholders (customers, suppliers, business partners etc.) need to think and work in ways conducive to making the changes sought by the strategy.

Looking back, I can see that I was working towards two things. A process for 'doing' strategy and a set of criteria to check if it had been done well (the Strategy Design Model gave rise to my first Strategy Design Checklist).[84]

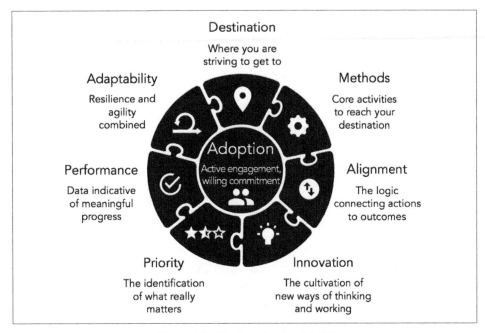

Figure 14. Strategy Design Model

Figure 15. The Strategy Lifecycle

In September 2020, I published *The Strategy Manual*,[85] which set out a clear framework for what 'doing' strategy actually meant. Strategy follows a three-stage lifecycle of strategy production, strategy adoption and strategy adaptation (Figure 15).[86]

Each of these stages involves very different types of strategy work, guided by different processes and informed by different tools and models:

1. **Strategy production:** This is where the strategy is invented, designed, crafted and brought to life. The strategy production stage is complete when the strategy is produced and launched. Strategy production has two core activities:

   a. **Strategy scoping** – Strategy scoping produces the 'brief' for strategy development. It summarises the main strategic opportunities and challenges and identifies the main drivers and aspirations for the new strategy. It also serves as a vital communication role across the organisation, by explaining simply and clearly what is going to be done in order to produce this strategy. Strategy scoping defines:

      i. What strategic change is sought – what is included in the strategy, and what is not;

      ii. How the strategy will be developed – who will do what by when, what evidence needs to be gathered and what decisions need to be made;

      iii. The acceptance criteria by which the new strategy, once written, will be judged good enough for launch.

   b. **Strategy development** – Strategy development is how you analyse, synthesise, imagine and commit to a new strategy, and how you write it and prepare it for dissemination throughout the organisation. Development involves the creative imagination of strategic ideas, informed by research and analysis, and validation of those ideas to ensure that the strategy you develop makes sense, has internal consistency and is conducive to adoption and adaptation.

2. **Strategy adoption:** The strategy adoption stage of the strategy lifecycle takes a completed written strategy and creates a delegated, scheduled, prioritised, measured and resourced plan necessary for its strategic success. It is where high-level, organisation-wide strategic goals are translated into actionable goals, applied to local circumstances, that front-line individuals and teams can achieve. Strategy moves from being owned by those who produced it, e.g. senior leadership, to being adopted by those who need to align behind it, e.g. most people in the organisation. It involves not just **planning** but **engagement and commitment,** i.e. securing active interest and a willingness to get involved. This is brought about by high levels of consultation, and by influence and autonomy being afforded to individuals and teams. The strategy adoption stage results in a strategic plan.

3. **Strategy adaptation:** Strategy adaptation is the cycle of sense-making, decision-making and change-making that keeps the organisation responsive to significant change. It involves both strategic resilience and agility, brought about by a combination of **measurement** and **governance**. The strategic plan you have at the end of strategy adoption, sadly, won't last long in its original form. The world will move on. Circumstances will change. And the plan will need to be adapted. If the plan changes so much it can no longer meaningfully derive from the strategy, it is time for a new strategy – strategic plans change but strategy doesn't. And if you are going to produce a new strategy, what better place to start than with a review of the current strategy? Strategy adaptation, therefore, ends with a strategy review.

In May 2022 I finally committed-to-print an idea that I'd been wrestling with for several years: that strategy is best thought of as a design thinking process.[87]

In simple terms, we can start to see strategy as three key stages of a design thinking process:

1. **Strategy sets out a design ambition** – inventing the future you want to bring about (note: strategy should never be about merely choosing the best available option);

2. **Strategy is managed by means of a design process** – iterative cycles of divergent and convergent thinking, progressively narrowing until we can define a desired destination or path;

3. **Strategy has two specific designed outputs** – the first is the production of a strategy that sets out the high-level goals by which our strategic ambition will be achieved; The second is a strategic plan setting out who does what, by when and to what standard in order to deliver the high-level strategic goals.

5.2 The strategy design process defined

In Chapter 2, we defined the key components of the design thinking process (see Section 2.5). To define the *strategy* design process, I have adapted these key components to apply to *strategic* thinking, as follows:

1. Strategy design is intentional or purposeful and, therefore, **the strategy design process begins by defining its intended outcome.** Often, this outcome will be defined in terms of a challenge that an organisation seeks to overcome. This challenge could be solving a problem or exploiting an opportunity. In different fields of strategy, the challenge could be functional (enabling part of an organisation to perform some function) or communicative (communicating a message or better articulating the brand). Typically, the desired outcome of strategy design is specified in a 'strategy scope' or a strategy scoping document (the 'brief' for the strategy).

2. In pursuit of this outcome, strategy design has four key characteristics:

    a. **The strategy design process is creative-by-nature.** This involves a cycle of:

        i. divergent thinking, which tries to imagine all possible ideas by which a bounded creative challenge could be met, and

        ii. convergent thinking, which involves creatively selecting, combining, hybridising and synthesising the ideas created in divergent thinking to find the best solutions to the given bounded, creative challenge.

b. **The strategy design process is iterative and progressively more narrowly-focused.** This involves repeated cycles of the divergent / convergent thinking process, but on each iteration, the bounded creative challenge has narrowed compared to the preceding cycle. So, whilst working on the conceptual principles of strategy, we seek to tackle a broad creative challenge – how in principle could we realise the aspirations set out in the strategy scope? However, after a preferred set of strategic principles have been agreed, strategy design will move on to tackle a narrower creative challenge – what are the specific, high-level strategic goals that could achieve the aspirations set out in the strategy scope?

c. **The strategy design process produces outputs that can be used to test the fitness-for-purpose of the strategy it has created.** Strategy design always produces an output at the end of its process (the strategy). The ultimate test of any strategy is whether it serves the purpose for which it was designed; does it achieve its intended aspirations, as set out in the strategy scope? In addition, strategy design typically produces an output at the end of each iteration of the strategy design process. This is used to check that progress towards fitness-for-purpose is being maintained and that drift, out-of-scope of the original strategy scope, is being avoided.

d. **The strategy design process is often non-linear.** Sometimes you will come up with a set of conceptual principles you think matches the strategy scope perfectly, until you move on to define the high-level strategic goals and you can't make it work. So, you loop back and come up with a different set of conceptual principles. Occasionally, you might also loop forward – how are the conceptual principles we've just come up with likely to land within the organisation? So, whilst the strategy design process, overall, can be seen as iterative and progressively more narrowly focused, the sequence of steps in that process is not simply sequential.

So far, this is 'merely' design thinking – it has all the key characteristics by which we defined design thinking previously.

But is strategy design 'deep design thinking'?

5.3 Strategy design as deep design thinking

In Chapter 4 we introduced deep design thinking as follows:

> A great deal of **design thinking** is about setting boundaries and maximising creativity within those boundaries.

> A great deal of **deep thinking** is about crossing boundaries and challenging boundaries. We explored how ecological thinking deepened, firstly by crossing into the disciplines of mathematics, genetics and animal behaviour and secondly by crossing over to very different domains of application. Studying planetary habitability and the gut microbiome are still applications of ecological thinking: they are still about the interactions of organisms and their environment. They are just very different organisms in very different environments.

> **Deep design thinking** BOTH sets boundaries AND challenges/ crosses boundaries as a core part of its process.

My view on strategy design is that it is almost impossible to do well without challenging and crossing boundaries. In my more fanciful moments I could even imagine strategy design becoming an epitome of deep design thinking. But I'm getting ahead of myself.

We talked of deep design thinking traversing boundaries from both a systems perspective and a stakeholder perspective. Let's explore these one at a time.

Strategy design from a systems perspective

A good strategy reaches from the top to the bottom of an organisation, and, in certain key regards, reaches beyond the organisation. Strategy is usually owned by the Board and is used to hold the CEO to account for the organisation's overall direction and performance. It should, therefore, be a prominent presence in the CEO's day-to-day working life and a tangible influence on their decision-making.

The power of that good strategy would, however, be greatly diminished if it never left the executive corridor. One of my favourite strategy stories that I've written about before[88] is Hornby Trains pivoting their strategy 20 years ago. They decided they no longer sold toys for kids and instead sold scale models for adult collectors. With that strategy-in-a-sentence they transformed the way everyone in the company thought about their jobs. Marketing and sales had new customers to focus on. Product designers had new criteria for choosing which product to develop next. Packaging designers had new features and qualities to highlight at point-of-sale. Beyond the company, new retail relationships needed to be established, new PR relationships with media outlets needed to be built and a whole new constituency of experts, enthusiasts and hobbyists needed to be engaged with. In five years, Hornby's share price increased over seven-fold.

Strategy design, therefore, needs to cross multiple system levels:

- The lived working experience of individual front-line team members;
- The functioning of parts of the organisation (e.g. teams, departments, business units);
- The operation and performance of the entire organisation;
- Relationships between the organisation and its external stakeholders;
- The global impact of the organisation and its activities (e.g. climate impact, pollution).

Strategy, as it develops, needs to be informed by people, data and insights from all of these system levels. Strategy, once completed, ought to inform and direct decisions and actions of people and groups at all these system levels.

Strategy design from a stakeholder perspective

Whilst this systems perspective requires taking many stakeholders' views into account, there is much more to the stakeholder perspective on strategy than this. Here are some of the key stakeholder perspectives that we haven't yet covered:

- **The leadership perspectiv**e – how do we lead the strategy design process? How do we make the strategy aspirational and stretching yet credible and attainable? How do we creatively imagine our future whilst keeping our creativity grounded in a robust evidence-base?

- **The data analyst perspective** – how do we portray the current circumstances of the organisation in ways that are conducive to strategy design? How do we evaluate strategy ideas to keep creative thinking in the Goldilocks zone – constrained enough to be focused yet not so constrained as to stifle innovative possibilities?

- **The finance perspective** – how do we meaningfully differentiate the financial imperatives that the strategy must achieve from the financial preferences we'd like the strategy to achieve? How do we project the costs of activities we've never undertaken before and how do we estimate revenue from services we haven't yet begun to develop?

- **The HR perspective** – how much change can the organisation accommodate within a given period of time? How do we performance-manage innovation? How much tolerance of failure is necessary in pursuit of innovation?

- **The 'community' perspective** – how much should staff across the organisation be involved in strategy design? How much should they be informed about the process, the decisions needed and the evidence base upon which these decisions will be made? To what extent should they be consulted about drafts of the strategy as it evolves?

So, strategy design needs to carve a complex navigational path through these different stakeholders.

Strategy design as deep design thinking – a worked example

Imagine we are a mid-sized commercial enterprise with a current strategy soon to expire. The Board has informed the CEO that they look forward to her proposed new strategy in six months' time. Her first task is to scope the new strategy. This will define the main strategic opportunities and challenges and identify its main drivers and aspirations. She decides that a three-year duration is the correct lifespan for the new strategy and sets her insights and analytics teams to work, producing projections and data packs for a forthcoming strategy scoping workshop with her senior leadership team. She is also aware that her front-line teams interacting directly with the outside world (customers, suppliers, partners) often have some of the best, real-time insights into the organisation's situation. She decides to take time to mine some of this raw data. She talks to sales teams to learn about prospects and competitors. She listens to customer support to hear about customers struggles and successes. She meets suppliers to hear about ways we could innovate across the entire supply-chain.

She has just challenged and crossed many boundaries in her strategic thinking. Originally, her boundaries were at their broadest: 'the future of the entire organisation'. She then narrowed these boundaries massively, whilst talking to front-line teams about their experiences with individual customers and prospects. Then came the hardest part. She had to expand her boundaries back to organisation-wide strategy and assimilate the knowledge she had gained at a whole different systems-level. When the customer service team told her about the struggle many small clients had in using one of their services, did this mean we, as an organisation, had issues with our usability design and usability-testing? When the enterprise sales team told the painful story of how they'd lost two of their biggest sales prospects at the last minute because a competitor had developed a feature that we had never even thought about, did this suggest that we were falling behind in our innovation?

As part of strategy scoping, the senior leadership team agreed on the main purpose of this new strategy. As a publicly listed company with large institutional shareholders, we need to achieve consistent profit margins at least as high as our sector competitors. In addition, since we have recently invested heavily in both staff recruitment and staff development, we seek to achieve these profit margins without having to reduce staff costs significantly. Finally, we need to progress our environmental credentials over the next three years, in particular reducing our carbon footprint.

With strategy scope defined, we have reached the first transition point in the strategy design process. We announce the start of strategy development to the organisation and open up communication channels for all staff to be able to make suggestions and offer ideas about the new strategy. Each member of the senior leadership team also discusses the detail of the strategy scope with their own leadership teams and passes their feedback to the CEO.

A few significant challenges to the strategy scope arise from this process. Several staff suggest we should have environmental and social ambitions beyond carbon emissions and the CEO decides to add a strategic review of our environmental and social governance to the strategy design process. Whilst it is broadly welcomed that cost reductions in staffing are not a strategic priority, it is suggested that cost reductions in other areas should be. The overall costs of our buildings and estate as well as our supply chain costs are highlighted. Again, the CEO adjusts the strategy scope to incorporate these ideas.

The revised strategy scope now defines the creative boundaries for the next stage of the strategy design process. The CEO sets each member of her senior leadership team the task of exploring all the possible changes the organisation could make over the next three years to maintain healthy levels of profitability, given the expected cost inflation, price erosion and the investment likely to be needed for environmental and social initiatives.

This next stage of the strategy design process produces many ideas for strategy, some of which could work in synergy together whilst others are in direct opposition to each other (e.g. invest heavily in innovation and launch lots of new services vs. double down on the refinement and optimisation of our existing services, whilst investing heavily in their marketing and sales). With some additional work, the strategy ideas are clustered and aggregated into a set of high-level strategic choices. To evaluate these, the CEO sets up two working groups. The first group is tasked with evaluating the defined high-level strategic choices within the strict framework of the strategy scope. The second group is tasked with exploring what might be missing from the defined strategic choices. Are there any radical, wild card, moon-shot ideas that ought to be considered as part of strategy design? It is this second group that makes strategy design a deep design thinking process. They are the ones to challenge and potentially cross the boundaries defined in the strategy scope.

The conclusion of this process is a further refined and developed strategy scope. It retains its core aim of 'market-expected levels of profitability', but some strategic options are accepted (investing heavily in innovation to develop new services) whilst others are rejected (investing heavily in marketing and sales of existing services).

There is also one 'boundary-crosser' that unexpectedly entered the realms of strategic possibility. Whilst the first working group was exploring the costs of modest improvements in carbon emissions, the second working group asked the question: 'How much would it cost to become fully carbon neutral in five years' time?' This crossed two boundaries. Firstly, it greatly exceeded the strategy scope which sought to 'make incremental improvements to our environmental credentials over the next three years, in particular reducing our carbon emissions'. It also exceeded the strategy lifespan, by exploring a five-year initiative for a three-year strategy. Despite this, it raised an interesting provocation: could we deliver a full solution to an issue (net zero carbon emissions) in five years instead of a partial and modest solution in three years?

So, by:

1. being aware of the system boundaries and the stakeholder boundaries within which strategy design operates;
2. using these boundaries constructively to focus creative strategic thinking without stifling it during divergent and creative thinking

cycles;

3. challenging these systems and stakeholder boundaries vigorously during the original strategy scoping process;

4. challenging these systems and stakeholder boundaries repeatedly at each transition point during the strategy design process

we get:

1. the rigour and structure of a design thinking process to help prevent strategy design descending into chaos;

2. the breadth of context and the depth of strategic innovation that comes from deep design thinking.

Baxter & Baxter

CHAPTER 6: Seaton's Journey - Ecological Design Thinking

The early years from 1960 to 1980

I must confess that in this period I didn't know anything about ecological design or ecological design thinking, although, on reflection, I believe our work at the Scottish Farm Buildings Investigation Unit (SFBIU) on 'animal welfare related design' came close to a philosophy of ecological design. In a report I wrote in 1969, entitled *"The Environmental Complex in Livestock Housing"*,[89] I used the definition of 'environment' as *"....the aggregate of all external conditions and influences affecting the life development of an organism"* and, when I extended it to 'the environmental complex', I can see its relationship to the current use of the term 'ecological' in design studies. There were also other signs of my tendency to move towards ecological design thinking. Later in this period I would contrast the conventional design perspective, which I called 'anthropocentric design', with a more animal-centred approach, which I called 'zoocentric design'. With plants, for example in the design of glasshouses in horticulture, I called this 'botanic centric design'.

Much later, in the period 2010 to 2020, with my colleague Fraser Bruce, Course Director in Product Design at the University of Dundee's Duncan of Jordanstone College of Art & Design (DJCAD), we would return to emphasise the teaching of this biocentric approach to design students in a paper entitled, *"Zoocentric Design: Pigs, Products, Prototypes and Performance."*[90] In addition, in the period up to the 1980s, 'animal welfare' became an important consideration in livestock production in the UK, whereas in the USA, 'animal rights' appeared more in popular debate. The combination of 'animal welfare' and 'animal rights' provided me with the incentive to explore the field of 'environmental ethics' and to get closer to the publications on ecological design. A final sign of my move towards environmental ethics can be found in my book *"Intensive Pig Production: Environmental Management and Design"*[91], which describes all of our technical studies related to pig production. In the Acknowledgements in this book there is the following quote, "*...and last but not least for whom it matters most, to pigs everywhere, whose behaviour has convinced me that there must be a better way.*" This further expresses my growing dissatisfaction with our technically dominated response to farm animal welfare.

Each of these tendencies moves me, the designer, closer to the boundaries of my current operating knowledge and beliefs. Ultimately, to make any progress, I have to cross the boundary and thereby extend and usually deepen my design thinking, for example from conventional anthropocentric design to zoocentric design to ecological design. Crossing the boundary from anthropocentric design to zoocentric design, to engage with a project involving non-human animals (farms, zoos, animal laboratories etc.), presents the following benefits:[92]

1. Good design could improve the wellbeing of all animals associated with humans and could improve animal/human performance.

2. It provides a different perspective (zoocentric) and a new challenge to design thinking.

3. It extends our understanding of other species and deepens our compassion for them.

4. It increases our awareness and knowledge of the impacts of our design and technological decisions on human/animal relationships.

5. It provides new sources of ideas and knowledge to stimulate imaginative thinking.

6. It raises questions of moral and ethical concern.

7. It provides one step towards a truly ecocentric natural design.

The Second Period from 1980 to 2000.

My pursuit of 'Ecological Design Thinking' (EDT) began in earnest in the early 1980s after resigning from the leadership of SFBIU in 1983. The latter years at SFBIU had left me with a new set of ambitions/tasks and a desire to extend what I had learned as a building surveyor operating in the exciting challenges of a rapidly changing field of agriculture and food production into the formal, higher education domain in which SFBIU had no remit. A paper I wrote then, titled *"Biology into Buildings"*,[93] although primarily about farm animal welfare and the design of buildings and equipment, also contained a deeper message about design and biology crossing each other's boundaries. This was an idea that would preoccupy me for the following several decades.

Fortunately, in the years from 1990 onwards, I had, as part of my continuing professional development, participated in several intensive 3-week residential courses at Schumacher College in Devon. These were unique, face-to-face learning experiences, and the most transformative for me were those taught by American pioneers in the emerging field of ecological design. People like John Todd, a Canadian biologist, his wife, the author Nancy Jack Todd, and David W Orr. Other courses featured outstanding teachers like James Lovelock and Stefan Harding on Gaia Theory, Arne Naess on Deep Ecology, Christian de Quincey on Radical Nature, Gregory Cajete on Native Science, Rupert Sheldrake on his New Science of Life and several others. This was 'mind bending' stuff and I was being appropriately 'radicalised' for a future we were about to enter then, and one we are in now. Thank you, Schumacher College.

Back in Aberdeen, I enrolled in an evening course at Aberdeen University on philosophy which specialised in environmental ethics, and I graduated in 1988 with a Postgraduate Diploma in Philosophy.

After leaving SFBIU in 1983, I became Head of the School of Surveying in the Robert Gordon Institute of Technology (RGIT), subsequently Robert Gordon University (RGU). With regard to achieving my ambitions on entering academia at RGIT, whilst these were slowed and hindered by Government changes in the financing of universities, it did provide the impetus for the development of new courses. A Building Surveying undergraduate Honours Degree was added to an existing Quantity Surveying Honours Degree to form a common core course approved by the Royal Institution of Chartered Surveyors (RICS). In addition, also encouraged by the RICS and in collaboration with the Department of Land Economy at Aberdeen University, we jointly launched an undergraduate Honours Degree in Marine Resource Management.

I raised the research profile of the School of Surveying by actively encouraging and supporting those members of staff who were both interested and capable of conducting good research and by building up a small cohort of PhD students. Most of this research effort was focused on rural developments in energy conservation and alternative means of developing alternative energy supply mainly through the capture and distribution of wind energy. We not only conducted research on the technologies but also on the impact these developments would have on the aesthetic qualities of the rural landscapes. Finally, with colleagues from other Schools/Departments in RGIT, we secured research funding from Historic Scotland, Scottish Homes and Gordon District Council, the Scottish Office and Scottish Natural Heritage. With regard to the School of Surveying's professional relationships, I was active on several committees of the RICS and an external examiner at four other Universities.

All of the above, took up several years of my time managing and growing the School of Surveying. However, I still found time to enlarge my practical and political environmental knowledge by engaging in the active support of organisations in the environmental field. For example, I became a Director in the Aberdeen Association for the Prevention of Cruelty to Animals; Chairman of Grampian Environmental Education Forum; President of Scottish Wildlife and Countryside Link; Chairman of The Deeside Forest, and Chairman of Scottish Outdoor Education Centres. All of these were voluntary unpaid posts. I was also very fortunate however to work (part paid) for Scottish Natural Heritage as Chairman of their North-East Board and a Member of their Main Board.

The work at RGIT/RGU was underlined and charged with my growing interest, knowledge and spirit of ecological design, which was eventually manifested in the design, development and launching of a Postgraduate Diploma / MSc in Ecological Design in 1993. This was a joint effort with my ex-colleagues in the Aberdeen School of Agriculture (biologists and ecologists) and my own staff, supported by visiting teachers in design and technology. The course was awarded several student scholarships from the European Union in the first few years of its operation. The structure of the course is shown in Table 1.

Table 1.
Course Structure for Postgraduate Diploma / MSc in Ecological Design (indicative only)

	SEMESTER 1				
WEEK	Monday	Tuesday	Wednesday (0.5 day)	Thursday	Friday
	PREPARATORY READING AS ADVISED				
1	ED01				
2	INTRODUCTION TO ECOLOGICAL DESIGN				
3	ED02		ED06 PROFESSIONAL SKILLS & RESEARCH METHODS (PART 1)	ED04	
4					
5	GEOLOGY, SOILS			APPLIED PHILOSOPHY	
6	& LANDSCAPES			& ETHICS	
7					
8					
9	ED03			ED05	
10					
11	NATURAL AND SEMI-			ECO-TECHNOLOGY	
12	NATURAL VEGETATION				
13					
14					
15	READING OR FIELD WEEK				

	SEMESTER 2				
WEEK	Monday	Tuesday	Wednesday (0.5 day)	Thursday	Friday
1	ED07		ED06 PROFESSIONAL SKILLS & RESEARCH METHODS (PART 2)	ED09	
2					
3	ECOLOGICAL			PLANNING &	
4	PROCESSES IN			DEVELOPMENT	
5	VEGETATION				
6					
7	ED08			ED10	
8					
9	VEGETATION			ENTERPRISE &	
10	CREATED BY MAN			INNOVATION	
11			CONFERENCE		
12					
13	ED11				
14	INTEGRATIVE SKILLS				
15	EXAMINATION				
	MINIMUM 18 WEEKS DISSERTATION				

POSTGRADUATE DIPLOMA

MASTERS DEGREE

The Aim of this course was:

"To introduce as many people of appropriate ability as possible to the concepts and consequences of ecological design so that they may pervade and ultimately influence as many academic, vocational, professional and recreational disciplines as possible in order to encourage and enhance the design, development and management of ecologically sustainable human actions."

Its objectives included:

- Appreciate and understand the philosophical and moral basis of human actions in relation to the wider environment;
- Think clearly and appropriately about the methods by which we secure knowledge prior to instigating action on the environment;
- Develop the knowledge and skills so that we have experience of information for use in natural and built environments;
- Use our knowledge wisely in our design and manipulation of technologies for use in natural and built environments;
- Develop our appreciation of the extent and means by which our developmental activities interact with the natural and social environment;
- Develop an understanding of the ways in which interactions between natural and built environments can be monitored and assessed;
- Use eco-systemic methods in the planning and design of future individual actions and sustainable communities;
- Develop, implement and manage sustainable enterprises of our own and others.

This was a bold venture in 1993 to introduce a more integrated, holistic design thinking approach to problem solving in a wide range of fields. The staff were all well qualified in the separate disciplines of ecology and design / technology and they were enthusiastic and fully committed to this new venture. The students too were enthusiastic and committed and they were all successful in graduating in the few years that the course was delivered. Whilst modular course structures, a prerequisite of new course approvals then, can have some administrative benefits, they tend to emphasise the 'parts' of the course rather than the integrated 'whole.' We overcame this impediment by using interactive face-to-face teaching, personal tutoring and the use of cross-boundary projects and assignments. The students responded well to these 'boundary dissolving' techniques by producing excellent imaginative essays, reports and, eventually, high-quality dissertations. For example, Anthony Lockey's dissertation *"Bioplex and Biomass Recycling - A Cure for Today's Waste Culture Tomorrow"*[94] was the study of an integrated waste management system for a local, small rural town. The coherent combination of theory and practice is essential to integration and to help students in the process of 'boundary crossing.' So, the course was ahead of its time by about 5-10 years! The university collaboration, however, did not have the patience or the resources to sustain a slow transition to a 'deeper understanding of ecological design', and this course no longer exists at RGU in Aberdeen.

Nevertheless, my involvement in this pioneering venture was to benefit my later associations with the Natural Design Group at Dundee in 1999 and with the MA in Ecological Design Thinking at Schumacher College in Devon in 2014.

Eventually, after a career as Professor, Assistant Principal / Dean, and Reader / Research Manager at RGU, I took retirement in 1997/98. So,15 years of exciting, adventurous and hard work managing and developing a School of Surveying culminated in formal retirement, an Emeritus Professorship, an OBE (in 1998) and, unfortunately at home, a divorce. The latter, an outcome of spending too much time working and not enough time with a growing family, was, in retrospect, a wrong decision.

The Third Period from 2000 to the Present, 2024.

After I formally retired from RGU (c. 1997/98) life slowed down a little. I went back to more hill walking and camping and married my second wife in 2004. She was also an ardent walker, camper and active environmentalist. In 1999 however, I was invited to take up a part-time Honorary Professorship at the School of Design in the University of Dundee to oversee and support the work of a small cohort of PhD students. I accepted the offer. From this small beginning, and with the support of Professor Tom Inns and Professor Georgina Follett, we secured two scholarships from the Student Awards Agency Scotland and the Arts and Humanities Research Council, and, with these two PhD students, we created 'The Centre for the Study of Natural Design' (CSND) or, in short, the Natural Design Group.

In 2005, I wrote a paper titled *"Deep Design and the Engineer's Conscience: A Global Primer for Design Education."*[95] The main title of the paper was compiled from the titles of two books, *"Deep Design"*[96] by David Wann and *"The Engineer's Conscience"*[97] by Meredith Thring. The intention of the paper was to prompt designers into new thinking which would help to resolve the problems described by Thring, which I had updated and reiterated, and to suggest that Wann's approach was a useful response. I also hinted that the PhD work we were engaged in at the Centre for the Study of Natural Design in Dundee was synonymous with Wann's 'deep design', and with 'ecological design' as he had pointed out in his earlier book titled *"Bio Logic: Designing with Nature to Protect the Environment"*.[98] In America, ten years earlier, ecological design had been clearly described by Nancy Jack Todd & John Todd[99] and was later fully explained by Nancy Jack Todd in her book *"A Safe and Sustainable World: The Promise of Ecological Design"*.[100] All of this work on ecological design was further explicated by David W. Orr in a number of books from 1992 onwards, i.e. *"Ecological Literacy"*,[101] *"Earth in Mind"*,[102] *"The Nature of Design"*[103] and *"Design on the Edge"*.[104] In the latter book, Orr describes the designing, developing and construction of the new Environmental Studies building at Oberlin College in 2000. This remarkable building, and its associated multidisciplinary teamwork, is a fine tribute to 'Ecological Design.' I was fortunate to be invited to the formal opening of this magnificent building and to meet David Orr again with his design team and some of his students. All of this background encouraged us to extend and deepen the knowledge base of ecological design at CSND and we called this 'natural design.'

At CSND we soon amassed a growing number of MSc and PhD scholars, most of whom contributed significantly to our deepening understanding and application of Natural Design (Ecological Design). In 2012, after ten years of successful operation, the University of Dundee had this to say about CSND in a promotional publication:

> "CSND's philosophy is 'deep sustainability' and it provides a platform for highly motivated post-graduate students, from any discipline, to challenge existing design perspectives, motivations and practices, and to actively debate and construct a way forward in the 21st century consistent with the new, emerging, alternative world-views. Students are attracted to the Group because they remain deeply dissatisfied with the many crises in today's world - climate change, pollution, loss of biodiversity, population growth and social inequity. These students are committed and dedicated to making a difference."

> "The (Natural Design) group offers a unique perspective on design. In particular, it sees it as an expanded activity beyond what currently constitutes the design domain and central to this is the need to develop a world in which nature and humankind co-operate as symbiotic, co-evolving living systems."

The similarity of this statement with the Aim of the MSc in Ecological Design delivered at the Robert Gordon University almost 20 years ago shows the continuity of thinking:

- The MSC in Ecological Design in Aberdeen sought to "encourage and enhance the design, development and management of ecologically sustainable human actions";

- The Natural Design Group in Dundee sought to "develop a world in which nature and humankind co-operate as symbiotic, co-evolving living systems".

Notwithstanding these similarities, here is a sample of the titles of successful PhD theses at Dundee all of which took their primary stimulus from the concept of 'Natural Design' whilst pursuing their own specific project and interests. This both widened and deepened our collective understanding and application of Natural Design.

- *"The Organics of Craft; The Influence of Goethe's Holism."* (PhD Thesis, Sandra Wilson, 2005)

- *"Designing in Dark Times: Modern Thought and the Nature of Design Knowledge."* (PhD Thesis, Barbara Brown, 2005)

- *"Design for Human and Planetary Health: A Holistic/Integral Approach to Complexity and Sustainability."* (PhD Thesis, Daniel Wahl, 2006)

- *"Co-Designing in Love: Towards the Emergence and Conservation of Human Sustainable Communities."* (PhD Thesis, Gonzalo Salazar Preece, 2011)

- *"Natural Design and Outdoor Learning: An Exploratory Case Study at Scottish Outdoor Education Centres."* (PhD Thesis, Fiona Wood, 2011)

- *"Holism and the Reconstitution of Everyday Life: A Framework for Transition to a Sustainable Society."* (PhD Thesis, Gideon Kossoff, 2011)

- *"Health, Food and Design Thinking."* (PhD Thesis, Steve Brogan, 2011)

- *"In the Making: An Exploration of the Inner Change of the Practitioner."* (PhD Thesis, Mona Nasseri, 2013)

- *"The Braided Way: Deep Democracy and Community."* (PhD Thesis, Gill Emslie, 2014)

- *"Symbiotic Design Practice: Designing With-In Nature."* (PhD Thesis, David Sanchez Ruano, 2016)

- *"Mindfulness-Based Design Practice."* (PhD Thesis, Kumanga Andrahennadi, 2019)

Several of these scholars are now in senior positions in many parts of the world and are promoting the vision and methods of ecological design.

Eventually my part-time post was terminated in 2012/13 and the Centre for the Study of Natural Design (CSND) was closed down.

So, maybe now 'real retirement' had arrived – but no! Soon after this retirement, I was invited by Schumacher College to lead their new MA in Ecological Design Thinking at Dartington in Devon. How could I refuse? I owe so much to Schumacher College and all the staff there, for their pioneering efforts in many fields including their MSc in Holistic Science and their short courses. It was a great joy to be able to reciprocate and for about two years I led, managed and taught this course. In my opinion, this was the first formal expression of the notion of Ecological Design Thinking. So, the progression looks something like this (Fig.16):

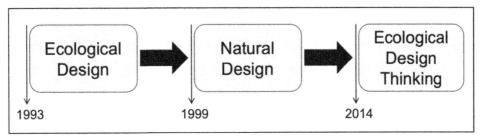

Figure 16. The progression of my thinking about Ecological Design Thinking

By 2014, Schumacher College and its collaborators had designed a postgraduate course in ecological design. After wise consultations, they called it an MA in Ecological Design Thinking. I was not involved in the design of this course, but I was invited, in 2014, to guide, manage and teach this bold venture. I did so with great pleasure and enjoyment working with the first two or three cohorts of students before deciding that I was now getting too old and that someone younger should now guide this great course.

For almost 10 years now Schumacher College has bravely and successfully pioneered ecological design thinking in the form of a Masters of Arts qualification. It has achieved this by its positive commitment to the subject and its resilience to the many challenges it has faced during this period. This educational model of ecological design thinking, in the form of an MA, will pause this year (2024) but a new model, more suited to new challenges, will be launched with many radical commitments to the College's belief in holistic education. The experience of 10 years with ecological design thinking will be absorbed as an integrating component of this new educational venture. This is a positive way forward for ecological design thinking. Once again, well done to Schumacher College and all its committed staff and students.

Seaton & Mike

References

[1] Baxter M, 1995. *Product Design: A Practical Guide to Systematic Methods of New Product Development.* Chapman & Hall, London.

[2] Baxter M, 2020. *The Strategy Manual: A step-by-step guide to the transformational change of anything.* Goal Atlas, London.

[3] Baxter M, 2023. *Core Values ... and how they underpin strategy & organisational culture.* Goal Atlas, London.

[4] https://en.wikipedia.org/wiki/Design

[5] https://en.wikipedia.org/wiki/St_Paul%27s_Cathedral

[6] https://en.wikipedia.org/wiki/Selimiye_Mosque,_Edirne

[7] https://en.wikipedia.org/wiki/Pyramid_of_Djoser

[8] Margolin V, 2005. A World History of Design and the History of the World. *Journal of Design History*, Autumn, 2005, Vol. 18, No. 3, The Global Future of Design History, Autumn, 2005, pp. 235-243

[9] van Schaik CP, Deaner RO and Merrill MY, 1999. The conditions for tool use in primates: implications for the evolution of material culture. *Journal of Human Evolution* (1999) 36, pp. 719–741.

[10] Pruetz JD and Bertolani P, 2007. Savanna Chimpanzees, Pan troglodytes verus, Hunt with Tools. *Current Biology*, March 2007, 17, pp. 412–417.

[11] https://simple.wikipedia.org/wiki/Negentropy

[12] http://www.snowcrystals.com/science/science.html

[13] Bejan A, 2019. *Freedom and Evolution: Hierarchy in Nature, Society and Science.* Springer, Switzerland.

[14] Alexander C, Ishikawa S and Silverstein M, 1977. *A Pattern Language: towns, buildings, construction.* Oxford University Press, New York.

[15] https://en.wikipedia.org/wiki/Design_pattern#Examples

[16] https://www.youtube.com/watch?v=IZefk4gzQt4

[17] Iouguina A, 2017. The Origin of Design: Designing the future by understanding the past. *Medium.com*, 7 Aug 2017.

[18] Proffitt T, Luncz L, Falótico, T et al, 2016. Wild monkeys flake stone tools. *Nature* 539, 85–88 (2016). https://doi.org/10.1038/nature20112

[19] Schmidt P, 2021. Steak tournedos or beef Wellington: an attempt to understand the meaning of Stone Age transformative techniques. *Humanities and Social Sciences Communications* 8, 280 (2021). https://doi.org/10.1057/s41599-021-00971-y

[20] The evolutionary origins of the octopus dates from over 300 million years. Larson C, 2022. Octopus ancestors lived before era of dinosaurs, study shows. https://phys.org/news/2022-03-octopus-ancestors-era-dinosaurs.html

[21] Finn JK, Tregenza T and Norman MD, 2009. Defensive tool use in a coconut-carrying octopus. *Current Biology,* Vol 19 No 23, 15 December 2009. https://doi.org/10.1016/j.cub.2009.10.052

[22] Nike Press release, 2023. *NIKE, INC. Reports Fiscal 2023 Fourth Quarter and Full Year Results.* https://s1.q4cdn.com/806093406/files/doc_financials/2023/q4/FY23-Q4-Combined-NIKE-Press-Release-Schedules-FINAL.pdf

[23] Newton G, 2004. Discovering DNA fingerprinting. *genome.wellcome.ac.uk,* February 2004. http://genome.wellcome.ac.uk/doc_wtd020877.html

[24] https://en.wikipedia.org/wiki/Human_evolution#Transition_to_behavioral_modernity

[25] Forty A, 1992. *Objects of Desire: Design and Society Since 1750.* Thames and Hudson Ltd, London. p. 36.

[26] Makov S, 2017. *Joy Paul Guilford – One of the founders of the Psychology of Creativity.* https://geniusrevive.com/en/joy-paul-guilford-one-of-the-founders-of-the-psychology-of-creativity/

[27] New World Encyclopedia, 2018 J.P. Guilford. https://www.newworldencyclopedia.org/entry/J._P._Guilford

[28] Baskerville R, Kaul M, Pries-Heje J, Storey VC and Kristiansen E, 2016. *Bounded Creativity in Design Science Research.* Proceedings of the 2016 International Conference on Information Systems (ICIS) cited at https://aisel.

aisnet.org/icis2016/ISDesign/Presentations/5/ and available online at https://aisel.aisnet.org/cgi/viewcontent.cgi?article=1141&context=icis2016

[29] The Goldilocks principle is explained on Wikipedia at https://en.wikipedia.org/wiki/Goldilocks_principle. Two Harvard Business Review articles have shown that creativity is boosted by constraints but hampered by too many. They are Richardson A, 2013. Boosting Creativity Through Constraints. *Harvard Business Review*, 11 June 2013 and Acar OA, Tarakci M and van Knippenberg D, 2019. Why Constraints Are Good for Innovation. *Harvard Business Review*, 22 November 2019.

[30] https://en.wikipedia.org/wiki/List_of_works_by_Leonardo_da_Vinci#Manuscripts

[31] The Design Council's Double Diamond https://www.designcouncil.org.uk/our-resources/the-double-diamond/

[32] Baxter M, 1995. *Product Design: A Practical Guide to Systematic Methods of New Product Development.* Chapman & Hall, London.

[33] Buchanan R, 1992. Wicked Problems in Design Thinking. *Design Issues*, Vol. 8, No. 2, (Spring, 1992), pp. 5-21. Quote from p 8.

[34] Brown T, 2008. Design Thinking. *Harvard Business Review*, June 2008.

[35] Papanek V, 1985. *Design for the Real World: Human Ecology and Social Change.* Thames and Hudson Ltd, London. p 3.

[36] Martin R, 2009. *Design of Business: Why Design Thinking is the Next Competitive Advantage.* Harvard Business Review Press, Boston.

[37] Simon HA, 1996. *The Sciences of the Artificial (3rd Edition).* The MIT Press, Boston.

[38] Simon HA, 1996. *The Sciences of the Artificial (3rd Edition).* The MIT Press, Boston. p 111.

[39] https://en.wikipedia.org/wiki/Ice_core#Antarctica_deep_cores

[40] https://en.wikipedia.org/wiki/Pi#Irrationality_and_normality

[41] https://en.wikipedia.org/wiki/Deep_learning

[42] https://en.wikipedia.org/wiki/Deep_learning#/media/File:Deep_Learning.jpg

[43] https://en.wikipedia.org/wiki/Lee_Sedol#Match_against_AlphaGo

[44] https://en.wikipedia.org/wiki/Lee_Sedol#Retirement_from_professional_play

[45] https://en.wikipedia.org/wiki/Google_Translate

[46] https://en.wikipedia.org/wiki/GPT-3

[47] https://en.wikipedia.org/wiki/GPT-4

[48] Egerton FN, 2001. A History of the Ecological Sciences: Early Greek Origins. *Bulletin of the Ecological Society of America*, January 2001. p 93.

[49] Elton C, 1927. *Animal Ecology*. The Macmillan Company, New York.

[50] MacArthur RH, 1958. Population Ecology of Some Warblers of Northeastern Coniferous Forests. *Ecology*, October 1958, 39(4), pp. 599-619.

[51] Hamilton WD, 1964. The genetical evolution of social behaviour. I. *Journal of Theoretical Biology*, Volume 7, Issue 1, 1964, pp. 1-16.

[52] Bull MJ and Plummer NT, 2014. Part 1: The Human Gut Microbiome in Health and Disease. *Integrative Medicine* (Encinitas), December 2014, 13(6), pp. 17-22.

[53] Stephen AM and Cummings JH, 1980. The Microbial Contribution to Human Faecal Mass. *Journal of Medical Microbiology*, Volume 13, Issue 1, 01 February 1990.

[54] https://en.wikipedia.org/wiki/Gut_microbiota

[55] https://en.wikipedia.org/wiki/Planetary_habitability

[56] https://en.wikipedia.org/wiki/Hypothetical_types_of_biochemistry

[57] Naess A, 1973. The shallow and the deep, long-range ecology movement: A summary. *Inquiry*, 16, pp. 95–100.

[58] Drengson A and Inoue Y, 1995. *The Deep Ecology Movement: An Introductory Anthology*. North Atlantic Books, Berkeley, California.

[59] Fox W, 1995. *Toward a personal ecology: developing new foundations for environmentalism*. Green Books Ltd, Totnes, Devon, pp. 91-92.

[60] Naess A, 1973. The shallow and the deep, long-range ecology movement: A

summary. *Inquiry*, 16, pp. 95–100.

[61] Naess A, 2008. *Life's Philosophy: Reason and Feeling in a Deeper World.* ATHENS, Georgia. University of Georgia Press.

[62] Roser M, 2024. Why is improving agricultural productivity crucial to ending global hunger and protecting the world's wildlife? Published online at *OurWorldInData.org*. Published online at https://ourworldindata.org/agricultural-productivity-crucial

[63] ibid

[64] Lal R, Reicosky DC and Hanson JD, 2007. Evolution of the plow over 10,000 years and the rationale for no-till farming. *Soil and Tillage Research*, Volume 93, Issue 1, 2007, pp.1-12.

[65] Hornbeck R, 2012. The Enduring Impact of the American Dust Bowl: Short- and Long- Run Adjustments to Environmental Catastrophe. *American Economic Review* 102 (4), June, pp.1477-1507.

[66] Allison R, 2020. How growers can help farming become carbon net zero. *Farmers Weekly*, 10 February 2020. Published online at https://www.fwi.co.uk/arable/land-preparation/soils/how-growers-can-help-farming-become-carbon-net-zero

[67] Nim Design. *What's so important about a brief?* Published online at https://nimdesign.com/why-do-you-need-a-good-design-brief/

[68] Sea Heft-Kniffin B, 2015. *Design Process: The Brief.* BrandiSea Design, 27 September 2015. Published online at https://www.brandisea.com/design-process-the-design-brief/

[69] Noel M. *How to Write a Design Brief.* Studio Noel. Published online at https://studionoel.co.uk/how-to-write-a-design-brief

[70] Chowdhury M, 2023. *Design Brief: What Is It & How to Make One (With Examples).* Windmill Digital. 16 August 2023. Published online at https://www.windmill.digital/design-brief-what-is-it-how-to-make-one-with-examples/

[71] Han E, 2022. What Is Design Thinking & Why Is It Important? *Harvard Business School Online*, Business Insights Blog, 18 January 2022. Published online at https://online.hbs.edu/blog/post/what-is-design-thinking

[72] Cameron LA, 2018. Agricultural Depression, 1920–1934. *MNopedia*,

Minnesota Historical Society. Published online at http://www.mnopedia.org/agricultural-depression-1920-1934

[73] *The Dust Bowl.* Episode One: The Great Plow-Up. Directed by Burns K, PBS, 18 November 2012. https://en.wikipedia.org/wiki/The_Dust_Bowl_(miniseries)

[74] https://en.wikipedia.org/wiki/Homestead_Acts

[75] A generic model of Design Thinking, inspired particularly by the Design Council's Double Diamond Model and Baxter (1995)'s Product design model but also from a variety of other design process models (see Dubberley 2008 https://www.dubberly.com/wp-content/uploads/2008/06/ddo_designprocess.pdf)

[76] https://quoteinvestigator.com/2014/05/22/solve/

[77] Hansen MT, 2010. IDEO CEO Tim Brown: T-Shaped Stars: The Backbone of IDEO's Collaborative Culture. *Chief Executive.* Published online at https://chiefexecutive.net/ideo-ceo-tim-brown-t-shaped-stars-the-backbone-of-ideoaes-collaborative-culture__trashed/

[78] Baxter M, 1995. *Product Design: A Practical Guide to Systematic Methods of New Product Development.* Chapman & Hall, London.

[79] https://www.linkedin.com/posts/mikebaxter_strategy-strategymanual-activity-6777890626772975616-iUhu/

[80] https://www.linkedin.com/pulse/essence-strategy-12-quotes-mike-baxter/

[81] Baxter M, 2019. University Strategy 2020: Analysis and benchmarking of the strategies of UK Universities. Goal Atlas, London.

[82] See the Strategy Design Model online at https://goalatlas.com/strategy-design-model/

[83] Drucker PF, 2012. *Management.* Routledge, p.114.

[84] See the Strategy Design Checklist online at https://goalatlas.com/strategy-design-model/

[85] Baxter M, 2020. *The Strategy Manual: A step-by-step guide to the transformational change of anything.* Goal Atlas, London.

[86] See the Strategy Lifecycle Model online at https://goalatlas.com/strategy-lifecycle-model/

[87] Baxter M, 2022. *Strategy Distilled May 2022*. Goal Atlas, London. Published online at https://goalatlas.com/strategy-distilled-may-2022/

[88] https://www.linkedin.com/posts/mikebaxter_strategy-strategymanual-activity-6785471286802960384-mCk2/

[89] Baxter SH, 1969. *The Environmental Complex in Livestock Housing.* Scottish Farm Buildings Investigation Unit, Craibstone, Aberdeen.

[90] Baxter SH, Bruce F, 2013. Zoocentric Design: Pigs, Products, Prototypes and Performance. *Proceedings of E&PDE 2013, the 15th International Conference on Engineering and Product Design Education, 2013.* pp. 672-677.

[91] Baxter SH, 1984. *Intensive Pig Production: Environmental Management and Design.* National Book Network, Lanham.

[92] Taken from: a) Baxter SH, 2006. The Way to Natural Design: Learning to See and Confront the Bigger Design Questions. *Enhancing Curricula: Contributing to the Future, Meeting Challenges of the 21st Century in the Disciplines of Art, Design and Communication.* 3RD CLTAD International Conference, Lisbon, Portugal, 6 -7 April 2006. Theme: The Ethical Curriculum: Designing Environmentally Responsible Curricula and b) Baxter SH, Bruce F, 2013. Zoocentric Design: Pigs, Products, Prototypes and Performance. *Proceedings of E&PDE 2013, the 15th International Conference on Engineering and Product Design Education,* 5 - 6 September 2013. pp. 672-677.

[93] Baxter SH, 1983. *Biology into Buildings* in Baxter SH, Baxter MR and MacCormack JAC (eds), 1983. *Farm Animal Housing and Welfare.* Martinus Nijhoff Publishers, The Hague.

[94] Lockey A, 1994. *Bioplex and Biomass Recycling - A Cure for Today's Waste Culture Tomorrow.* PhD Thesis, University of Dundee.

[95] Baxter SH, 2005. Deep design and the engineer's conscience: a global primer for design education. *Crossing design boundaries: proceedings of the 3rd Engineering & Product Design Education International Conference*, Edinburgh, UK, 15-16 September 2005.

[96] Wann D, 1995. *Deep Design: Pathways To A Livable Future.* Island Press, Washington, D.C.

[97] Thring MW, 1980. *The Engineer's Conscience.* Northgate Publishing Co. Ltd., London.

[98] Wann D, 1994. *Bio Logic: Designing with Nature to Protect the Environment.* Johnson Books, Michigan.

[99] Todd NJ and Todd J, 1984. *Bioshelters, Ocean Arks, City Farming; Ecology as the Basis of Design.* Sierra Club Books, San Francisco.

[100] Todd NJ, 2005. *A Safe and Sustainable World: The Promise of Ecological Design.* Island Press, Washington, D.C.

[101] Orr DW, 1992. *Ecological Literacy: Education and the Transition to a Postmodern World.* SUNY press, Albany.

[102] Orr DW, 2004. *Earth in Mind: On Education, Environment, and the Human Prospect.* Island Press, Washington, D.C.

[103] Orr DW, 2004. *The Nature of Design: Ecology, Culture, and Human Intention.* Oxford University Press, USA.

[104] Orr DW, 2006. *Design on the Edge: The Making of a High–Performance Building.* MIT Press, Boston.

Printed in Great Britain
by Amazon

44558056R00064